engaging the government to regulate online and social media corporations, though meaningful regulations are rarely instituted. Individuals will have to protect themselves and their families, and I appreciate how this book exposes the problem and provides useful remedies.

—CK Westbrook, author of *The Impact Series*

I0090170

DISCONNECTED
TOGETHER

DISCONNECTED
TOGETHER

A Family's Guide to Reclaiming Connection in a Digital World

Harry Gill, MD, PhD
Karyne E. Messina, EdD, FABP

Disconnected Together
PI Press, Chevy Chase, MD

Book design by Vinnie Kinsella, Paper Chain Book Publishing Services

ISBN 978-1-7362388-5-1 (paperback)
ISBN 978-1-7362388-6-8 (ebook)

Acknowledgments

Dr. Harry Gill

I would like to thank my love, friend, husband, and partner in everything I do, Paul Gill, without whom this book would not be possible. His never-ending support and patience with me are a constant source of comfort. I also wish to thank both of my children, Sebastian and Oleon, as I've learned much of what I wrote about in this book by observing their development. They are amazing and continue to inspire my love of life and love.

Last but not least, I express my deepest gratitude to Ariana Bulgarelli, who was not only my sounding board while formulating the ideas for this book, but has also been instrumental in helping convert my writing as a neuroscientist and non-native English speaker into the text that is in front of you.

Dr. Karyne Messina

It is my pleasure to thank the people who made this book possible. First and foremost, I am grateful for my husband and best friend, Gary. His unwavering support has been invaluable. To my cherished daughters, Ann-Kathryn and Kiki, thank you for your legal guidance and for being there for me every step of life's journey.

I am also deeply indebted to my parents, whose insistence on teaching us honor, courage, and integrity has been a guiding light in my own life and work. My grandchildren—Isabel, Olivia, Chris, and

Ayla—have been a constant source of wonder and insight, offering a real-world perspective on the beautiful journey of human development.

Finally, a heartfelt thank you to Dr. Gill and to everyone else who contributed to the creation of this book.

Contents

Preface...1
Introduction..3
Note to Parents and Educators 7

Part 1: Infants and Young Children (0–7 Years)
Chapter 1: Where Is Mother?..................................11
Chapter 2: The Hijacking of Play and Language.....................19
Chapter 3: When the Interpreter Is Preoccupied 27
Chapter 4: Forging the Self Amid the Static 35

Part 2: The Tween and Adolescent Years (8–18)
Chapter 5: The Adolescent Brain on Screens..........................45
Chapter 6: The Search for Self.....................................53
Chapter 7: The Vanishing Interior 61
Chapter 8: The Game of Thrones 69
Chapter 9: The Overwhelmed Ego................................. 77
Chapter 10: The Shattered Mirror 85
Chapter 11: Phantoms in the Machine............................93
Chapter 12: When the Screen Turns Deadly 101
Chapter 13: The Shared Psychosis 109

Part 3: Adulthood and Aging
Chapter 14: The Adult in the Machine 117
Chapter 15: The Plastic Brain....................................... 125
Chapter 16: Reclaiming Our Minds 131
Chapter 17: The Aging Brain....................................... 139

Chapter 18: The Double-Edged Screen 145
Chapter 19: The Search for Integrity vs. Despair 153

A Call To Action 159
Part 1 Toolkit 161
Part 2 Toolkit 165
Part 3 Toolkit 173

Conclusion 179
Epilogue 181

Preface

Day after day, in our respective clinical practices, Dr. Messina and I found ourselves listening to the same story. The details varied—different people, different words, different life stages—but the underlying theme was unnervingly consistent. It was a story of disconnection.

We heard it in an anxious teenager who felt an unrelenting pressure to perform online yet could not tolerate five minutes alone with his own thoughts. We saw it in a couple in their forties, sitting on opposite ends of a couch, describing a marriage hollowed out by the silent glowing screens that had become their constant companions in bed. It was there in the high-functioning executive who felt his attention span was "shot," unable as he was to stay with a single task without the reflexive urge to check his email. And it was present in the grieving widower in his seventies who confessed that his only remaining sense of connection came through the flickering images on his television.

As a psychiatrist with a PhD in neuroscience and a psychoanalyst, we began to see a common thread running through these struggles. The presenting problems were varied: anxiety, depression, addiction, marital conflict, loneliness. The backdrop was the same: a world saturated with digital technology. It became clear that we were not just treating isolated cases. We were witnessing a profound shift in the human experience, one that was reshaping our patients' brains, their relationships, and their sense of self in ways we were only beginning to understand.

We wrote this book to connect the dots. Our goal is to unite two powerful but often separate ways of understanding the human mind. Neuroscience gives us the "how." It reveals how the brain's reward systems are hijacked by social media, how neural circuits for empathy can atrophy from disuse, and how the architecture of a child's brain is physically shaped by the presence or absence of an attuned caregiver. Psychoanalysis gives us the "why." It provides a deep and nuanced language for understanding the meaning of these changes, illuminating how they alter our internal world, our defenses, and our fundamental capacity for love and connection.

This book is the result of that synthesis. It is our attempt to provide a clear, comprehensive guide to the psychological and neurological effects of screen time across the human lifespan. It is, however, not an anti-technology manifesto. Rather, it is an argument for humanity: a call to awareness, a map for navigating this new terrain, and a testament to the fact that connection, presence, and intimacy are not luxuries but essential nutrients for a healthy mind. Our greatest hope is that by understanding the forces at play, each of us can begin to make more conscious, intentional choices in the way we live our lives, both on and off the screen.

Introduction

One only needs to witness a child harmed by social media to understand, at a deeply emotional level, that the ways our digital devices shape our lives and distort our view of reality can be a matter of life and death. During Senate Judiciary Committee hearings on child safety in January 2024, the country saw firsthand the raw pain of parents whose children had suffered or died in ways undeniably linked to social media: children driven to self-harm after relentless online bullying, extorted or sexually exploited through apps, or who accidentally overdosed on drugs obtained via Snapchat. While most agree that social platforms are harmful to kids, the damage is not limited to children and teens.

As a psychiatrist and a psychoanalyst, we contend almost daily with one of the greatest harms facing our patients of all ages today: the profound effect digital devices have on the brain and the mind. This is not a niche problem. It is the defining challenge of life in the 21st century.

Our ceaseless digital interactions—through social media, multiplayer games, and the endless scroll—are haunting reminders of how rapidly life is changing. We are bombarded with constant stimulation yet becoming more distant and isolated from one another in the analog world than ever before. Our patients' individual tragedies, addictions, and hollowed-out interpersonal lives are a microcosm of the problem we all face as misinformation spreads and social structures fracture on a global scale.

Much of our clinical experience involves untangling how people perceive reality and the sources they use to construct it. When you recognize that "reality" is first negotiated between our neurons and then renegotiated between people, it becomes clear how our shared sense of what is real has eroded. Consider the attempted assassination of a former U.S. President on July 13, 2024. In real time, smartphones erupted with push alerts, graphic videos, and conspiracy theories. With thousands of attendees recording on their phones, the event became one of the most documented assassination attempts in history. It also became one of the most fractured in terms of shared understanding.

This book is not about hypothetical situations. Babies are born into this hyperactive, manipulated digital world every day, and the rest of us are aging into it. The water we swim in is already at its boiling point. Are we, like the proverbial frogs, unaware of the danger?

Disconnected Together is organized according to the stages of development laid out by psychologist Erik Erikson. Drawing on our clinical experiences and our expertise in neuroscience and psychology, we take readers on a tour of Erikson's stages of life, from infancy to old age. At each stage we face unique modern challenges brought on by screen time, challenges Erikson could never have imagined. Yet we find his framework more powerful now than ever. If we are capable of further development at every stage of life, and if adult experiences can help heal the harms of childhood, then there is always hope. With work and care the damage can be undone.

In the span of a single lifetime, the definition of "screen time" has fundamentally changed. In the 1960s it meant the family television. By the 1980s and 1990s it was the 24-hour news cycle, bringing national tragedies into our living rooms and classrooms. But at least we always had the option of turning the TV off.

The pivot point came with the smartphone. As comedian Bo Burnham (2021) sang, *It was always the plan to put the world in your hand.* In the early 2000s, humanity created technology that our brains were not evolved to handle. The algorithms that drive content are no longer simple sorting tools. They are sophisticated, personalized mechanisms designed to drive engagement by exploiting our brain's natural reward systems (Trifiletti & Gore, 2022). This is the genie in the bottle, and keeping a force with the power of instant wish fulfillment close at hand rarely works out in humanity's favor.

The platforms that claim to connect us are often the very source of our extreme isolation.

This is not simply the slow social drift chronicled in Robert Putnam's *Bowling Alone* (2000). It is a new world, remade in the image of social platforms, and it is the only world most of Generation Z and all of Generation Alpha have ever known.

This book is written for adolescents, parents, educators, researchers, health professionals, and anyone concerned with the perils of our digital lives. We aim to help readers become conscious of science-informed choices that make it possible to reconnect with the people and experiences that matter in the physical world. While we call for government initiatives to protect people from the dangers of excessive screen time, we are not willing to wait for policy to catch up. We are not Luddites. We are defenders of the here and now, of the full human spectrum of emotion and experience.

We hold this as a fundamental principle: the only thing we have is time, and the only thing we need is kindness and love. Social media and the unending stream of content were designed to devour our time and our minds. They condition us to accept the palest ad-fueled algorithm-manipulated imitations of love—the fleeting validation of a "like" in place of a physical embrace—as though they were the real thing.

Introduction References

Burnham, B. (2021). *Welcome to the Internet.* [Song]. On *Inside (The Songs).* Imperial Distribution.

Putnam, R. D. (2000). *Bowling alone: The collapse and revival of American community.* Simon & Schuster.

Trifiletti, E., & Gore, L. (2022). The psychology of social media. In *The Cambridge handbook of the psychology of social issues.* Cambridge University Press.

Note to Parents and Educators

This book is divided into four parts, each corresponding to an age group across the human lifespan. Our aim is to help people of all ages understand what can be done to address the challenges that arise from excessive screen time. The material is presented both through a neuroscientific lens and a psychoanalytic lens so that readers can see how biology and psychology interact to shape our experiences.

To make the book easy to use, each chapter concludes with a **What Can Be Done?** section that offers clear, practical tips for the age group under discussion. These recommendations are designed not only for parents and educators, but also for clinicians, policymakers, and anyone seeking guidance.

Following this, every chapter includes a **Chapter Highlights** section, which distills the most important takeaways into three categories:

- Key Concepts that summarize the central ideas of the chapter
- Key Neuroscience Concepts that highlight the relevant findings from brain science
- Key Psychoanalytic Concepts that explain the inner psychological processes at work

Finally, at the end of the book, readers will find **Toolkits**. These toolboxes gather strategies, resources, and applications that expand on the material in the chapters and provide additional support for putting ideas into practice.

Our hope is that this structure makes the book both comprehensive and accessible.

Whether you read it straight through or turn directly to the section that applies to your current stage of life as a child, student, or parent, you will find both practical guidance and a deeper understanding of how screens shape our minds, our relationships, and our development.

PART 1

Infants and Young Children (0–7 Years)

Where Is Mother?

Prolonged Exposure to Screen Time Through the Lenses of Neuroscience and Attachment Theory

The Brain's Story: Early Neural Development

Modern neuroscience now provides a stunningly detailed map of how early experiences shape a child's brain. An infant is born with a brain full of potential but without a coherent structure. The prefrontal cortex (PFC), the brain's "mission control" for planning and emotional regulation, is particularly malleable. At birth it contains billions of neurons that are richly interconnected. Through a process called synaptic pruning, experiences with the environment strengthen the connections that are used and eliminate those that are not (Huttenlocher & Dabholkar, 1997).

Which connections are preserved depends on the infant's interactions. The back-and-forth exchanges known as "serve and return"—such as a parent's smile in response to a baby's coo—are the building blocks of social and emotional intelligence. These micro-interactions literally sculpt the brain. The process is accelerated by myelination, in which a fatty sheath coats the axons of neurons, allowing for faster and more efficient communication between brain regions (Asato et al., 2010). In this way, rich real-world interactions serve as the raw materials for the brain's essential construction project, laying the foundation for future learning, empathy, and resilience.

The Indispensable Caregiver: A Psychoanalytic View

Imagine a tiny explorer, newly arrived in a world bursting with sensory input. Every sound is a symphony, every touch a revelation, every face a universe waiting to be understood. This miniature being possesses an innate drive to connect, to make sense of experience, and to organize the overwhelming chaos of the new. Ideally that drive is met by a loving, attuned caregiver: a beacon of predictability and warmth who serves as a living guide to reality. This is the crucible of early development, a delicate dance of responsiveness and unfolding understanding in which the foundations of self, emotion, and relationship are forged.

Pioneering psychoanalysts grasped this instinctively. Melanie Klein (1952) proposed that the first year of life provides a template for all that follows. She argued that an infant's sense of self is shaped through interactions with the primary caregiver, with early experiences of love and frustration forming the inner world. Heinz Kohut (1971) emphasized the development of a healthy self, which depends on what he called "self-object" relationships in which caregivers provide empathy and validation. He believed that a child must feel seen and admired in order to build a stable sense of identity. Donald Winnicott (1964), both pediatrician and psychoanalyst, offered the enduring idea of the "good-enough mother," a caregiver who provides safety but also allows manageable frustrations that help the infant develop resilience.

Perhaps most influential were John Bowlby (1969) and Mary Ainsworth (1978), who established attachment theory and demonstrated that a baby's need for a secure bond with a caregiver is a primary motivational force, as essential as food or shelter. In the presence of an attached parent, a child can explore the world with confidence, knowing that a safe harbor is close by. Erik Erikson (1950) extended this idea into his stages of psychosocial development, noting that it is through consistent, responsive care that an infant develops basic trust—the foundational belief that the world is a safe and reliable place.

Though their language and frameworks differ, these theories converge on a single truth: the consistent, emotionally available presence of a caregiver is the most critical ingredient for healthy psychological development. Without it, the child's sense of trust, resilience, and identity is built on unstable ground. With it, the child gains the secure base needed to flourish.

When the Caregiver is Distracted

So what happens when the caregiver, the architect of the infant's developing brain and mind, is consistently distracted by a "portable electronic pacifier"? The entire developmental process is placed at risk. From a psychoanalytic perspective, the distracted caregiver cannot be good enough. They cannot provide the consistent mirroring that Kohut described, leaving the child feeling unseen.

They cannot create the "secure base" Bowlby and Ainsworth identified as essential for exploration. The infant's bids for connection go unanswered, and the foundation of trust Erikson described begins to crumble, replaced by mistrust and anxiety. The child is left in what might be called a disorienting position: alone, dazzled by the lights of a screen, but without a human guide to help make sense of it all.

Neuroscience research validates this concern with alarming clarity. Studies using the "still-face" paradigm, in which a parent suddenly becomes unresponsive, show that infants react with immediate distress, confusion, and withdrawal (Tronick, 1989). A parent absorbed in a phone re-creates a series of still-face moments throughout the day. This phenomenon, now termed "technoference," reduces parent-child verbal and nonverbal interactions, diminishes parental responsiveness, and often produces negative exchanges, such as irritation when the child interrupts (McDaniel & Radesky, 2018).

For the developing brain, the consequences are direct. Passive screen viewing does not engage neural circuits in the same way human interaction does. Research shows that excessive screen time in infancy is linked to language delays, attention problems, and poorer executive function later in childhood (Madigan et al., 2019). The brain is being wired for distraction instead of for the focused, reciprocal communication it needs in order to thrive. In plain terms, handing a baby a tablet at dinner may keep them quiet, but it also compromises their brain development.

What Can Be Done?

The picture we've painted is concerning, but it is not without hope. The goal is not to demand perfection from parents, which is impossible, but to foster awareness and intentionality. Here are practical strategies to protect the crucial parent-infant bond in the digital age.

- **Create Tech-Free Zones and Times.** Designate certain times of the day as sacredly screen-free. The most important are feeding times (breast or bottle), diaper changes, and bedtime routines. These are prime moments for eye contact, touch, and bonding that should not be interrupted. Make the infant's play area a phone-free zone.
- **Prioritize "Serve and Return."** The most powerful engine of brain development is the "serve and return" interaction. When a baby "serves" by cooing, pointing, or making a facial expression, parents should "return the serve" by responding in a meaningful way. This is the foundation of communication. Put the phone down, get on the floor, and be an active play partner.
- **Narrate Your Day.** Even when you're busy with chores, talk to your baby. Describe what you're doing, what you see, and what they see. This constant stream of language is a rich source of neural nourishment, even if the infant doesn't understand the words. It demonstrates presence and engagement.

- **Mindful Phone Use.** When you do need to use your phone, try to do it when the baby is safely occupied or asleep. If you must use it in their presence, explain what you are doing. Saying, "I'm just sending a quick message to Grandma" is better than silent, absorbed scrolling. This models that technology is a tool with a purpose, not an all-consuming escape.
- **Audit Your Own Habits**. It's crucial for parents to reflect on *why* they are reaching for their phones. Is it boredom? Stress? A need for connection? Finding alternative coping strategies—like taking a few deep breaths, stretching, or stepping outside for a moment—can reduce the reflexive urge to escape into a screen.
- **For Professionals.** Pediatricians, therapists, and childcare providers should make conversations about technoference a routine part of their care. Ask parents about their screen-time habits in a nonjudgmental way. Provide them with the resources and the "why" behind limiting screen exposure for infants and for themselves. Emphasize that the parent's presence is the most valuable developmental "toy" their child will ever have.

Key Neuroscience Concepts

- *Prefrontal Cortex (PFC):* Often called the brain's "CEO," this region is responsible for high-level executive functions like impulse control, planning, and emotional regulation. Its prolonged development (through adolescence) makes it uniquely vulnerable to the quality of early life experiences.
- *Synaptic Pruning:* The brain's "use it or lose it" process. An infant's brain has an overabundance of neural connections (synapses). The experiences and interactions a child has strengthen the connections that are used, while those that are neglected are "pruned" away. This makes early relational experiences the primary architect of the brain's mature structure.
- *Myelination:* The process by which nerve fibers are coated with a fatty sheath called myelin, which acts like insulation on a wire. Myelination dramatically increases the speed and efficiency of communication between brain regions and is essential for the development of coordinated thought and complex skills.
- *"Serve and Return":* The term for the simple back-and-forth interactions that are the building blocks of a healthy brain. When an infant "serves" (with a gaze, a coo, or a gesture) and a caregiver "returns" (with an attuned smile, a word, or a touch), it builds and strengthens the neural circuits for communication, emotional regulation, and all future learning.

Key Psychoanalytic Concepts

- *Attachment Theory (Bowlby & Ainsworth):* The foundational theory that an infant has an innate biological need to form a strong emotional bond with at least one primary caregiver. This bond provides a "secure base" from which the child can safely explore the world and a "safe haven" to return to in times of distress.

- *The "Good-Enough" Mother (Winnicott):* The concept that effective mothering is not about being perfect but about being consistently and reliably present and attuned to the infant's needs. The "good-enough" caregiver provides a "holding environment" that feels safe but also allows for small, manageable frustrations that help the child develop resilience and a sense of self separate from the parent.

- *Mirroring (Winnicott & Kohut):* The vital process in which the caregiver's responsive face acts as a mirror, reflecting the infant's internal emotional state back to them. This experience of being "seen" and understood allows the infant to organize their feelings and develop a cohesive sense of self.

- *Trust vs. Mistrust (Erikson):* The first and most fundamental crisis of psychosocial development. Through consistent, loving, and responsive care, the infant learns to trust that the world is a safe and reliable place. Inconsistent or neglectful care can lead to a foundational sense of mistrust that can affect relationships throughout life.

Chapter 1 References

Ainsworth, M. D. S., Blehar, M. C., Waters, E., & Wall, S. (1978). *Patterns of attachment: A psychological study of the strange situation*. Lawrence Erlbaum.

Asato, M. R., Terwilliger, V., Woo, J., & Luna, B. (2010). White matter development in adolescence: a DTI study. *Cerebral Cortex, 20*(11), 2654–2661.

Bowlby, J. (1969). *Attachment and loss, Vol. 1: Attachment. Attachment and Loss*. New York: Basic Books.

Erikson, E. H. (1950). *Childhood and society*. W. W. Norton & Company.

Huttenlocher, P. R., & Dabholkar, A. S. (1997). Regional differences in synaptogenesis in human cerebral cortex. *The Journal of Comparative Neurology, 387*(2), 167–178.

Klein, M. (1952). Some theoretical conclusions regarding the emotional life of the infant. In *Developments in psycho-analysis* (pp. 198–236). Hogarth Press.

Kohut, H. (1971). *The analysis of the self: A systematic approach to the psychoanalytic treatment of narcissistic personality disorders*. University of Chicago Press.

Madigan, S., Browne, D., Racine, N., Mori, C., & Tough, S. (2019). Association between screen time and children's performance on a developmental screening test. *JAMA Pediatrics, 173*(3), 244–250.

McDaniel, B. T., & Radesky, J. S. (2018). Technoference: Parent distraction with technology and associations with child behavior problems. *Child Development, 89*(1), 100–109.

Tronick, E. Z. (1989). Emotions and emotional communication in infants. *American Psychologist, 44*(2), 112–119.

Winnicott, D. W. (1964). *The child, the family, and the outside world*. Penguin Books.

The Hijacking of Play and Language

How Screens Reshape Critical Early Skills

Our brains are not built in a quiet factory. They are constructed on the bustling, unpredictable playground of life. The foundational wiring of the prefrontal cortex, with its processes of synaptic pruning and myelination described in the previous chapter, does not unfold in isolation. It is driven by a child's direct multisensory engagement with the world. Two of the most powerful engines of this development are play and language. These are not simply pastimes for a young child; they constitute the essential work of building a mind.

This chapter explores how excessive and passive screen time can hijack these fundamental processes, redirecting the trajectory of a child's cognitive and emotional growth. What should be a symphony of discovery and connection risks becoming a flat, one-dimensional echo of real experience.

The Power of Play: Building a World from the Inside Out

Before a child can understand complex social rules or academic concepts, they must first understand the physical world and their place within it. This is the magic of unstructured play.

When a toddler stacks blocks, they are not just making a tower; they are conducting a hands-on physics experiment in gravity and balance. When a child engages in pretend play, perhaps caring for a doll or flying to the moon in a cardboard box, they are developing critical skills in creativity, problem-solving, empathy, and emotional regulation. This type of play, driven by the child's own curiosity, builds the neural pathways for flexible, adaptive thinking.

Passive screen time offers the opposite. Instead of being an active creator, the child becomes a passive recipient of prepackaged stimulation. The vibrant, fast-paced content is captivating but requires little to no internal effort. Research increasingly shows that heavy screen use in early childhood is associated with a reduced capacity for imaginative play and creativity. Children may learn to expect entertainment to be delivered *to* them rather than generating it themselves. This can stifle the development of an inner world, the rich landscape of imagination from which so much of our adult identity and resilience grows. A 2019 study in *JAMA Pediatrics* found that higher screen time in children aged two to three was associated with poorer developmental outcomes at ages 3 and 5, highlighting how early habits can have lasting consequences.

The Roots of Language: A Conversational Dance

Language is not learned from flashcards or educational apps; it is absorbed through the rich, messy, back-and-forth dance of human conversation. This process, known as "serve and return," is the bedrock of communication. A baby babbles, a parent responds with words and a smile. A toddler points at a dog and a caregiver says, "Yes, that's a big fluffy dog!" This dance relies on what developmental psychologists call "joint attention"—the shared focus of two individuals on an object. It is through joint attention that words become linked to the world, and communication becomes meaningful.

Screens, especially when used by a child alone, shatter this interactive model. A screen cannot engage in joint attention. It cannot notice when a child is confused or excited. It cannot tailor its response to the child's unique cues. Consequently, studies have consistently linked high levels of screen time in infants and toddlers to expressive language delays. For every 30-minute increase in daily handheld screen time, one study found a 49% increased risk of expressive speech delay (Birken et al., 2017). The brain is being wired to receive auditory information passively, not to engage in the active reciprocal process of conversation that is essential for robust language development.

Furthermore, observing adult interactions and conversations provides the developing brain with essential building blocks for future relationships with peers and adults. Modulation of tone, changes in the rate of speech, and the facial expressions used during discussion, problem-solving, or even casual gossip all serve as rich learning material. When a child is handed a screen, or when adults are absorbed in their own screens instead of communicating, that vital learning opportunity is lost. The destructive impact of this absence is unmistakable.

Building the Brain's CEO: Executive Functions

Executive functions are a set of high-level mental skills housed in the prefrontal cortex. They include working memory (holding information in mind), impulse control (thinking before acting), and cognitive flexibility (shifting between tasks or perspectives). These abilities form the backbone of learning and self-regulation, and they are built gradually through real-world experience. Waiting your turn in a game strengthens impulse control. Following multistep directions to bake cookies exercises working memory. Such activities require children to manage attention, regulate behavior, and think ahead.

Screens undermine this process. Most digital content is designed for instant gratification, offering rewards without the effort that builds control. All digital content is designed for continued engagement through an unrelenting stream of visual and auditory stimulation. Rapid scene changes in much of the content designed for children can overwhelm a young child's attention system rather than strengthen it. A study at the University of Bath (2021) found that toddlers with high daily touchscreen use were quicker to notice objects when they appeared but were also more easily distracted than their peers with little or no touchscreen use. In effect, their brains were being trained for reactivity, not for the sustained, focused attention that supports deep learning and long-term self-regulation.

Play and language are the natural training grounds for executive function. When these are displaced by passive screen time, children lose the very experiences that wire the brain for patience, persistence, and flexible problem-solving.

What Can Be Done?

Protecting and nurturing a child's development in the digital age is not about eliminating technology but about fiercely prioritizing the real-world interactions that build a healthy brain.

- **Champion Unstructured Play.** Create a "yes space" where your child is safe to explore. Stock it not with electronic toys that have a single function but with open-ended items like blocks, dress-up clothes, art supplies, and cardboard boxes. Importantly, join in their play but let them lead. Follow their narrative, become a character in their story, and resist the urge to direct the action. Your engaged presence validates their imaginative world.
- **Become a "Sportscaster" for Their Day.** Narrate the world for your child. "I'm washing the red apple now. Can you feel how smooth it is?" "Look at that big truck driving by! It's so loud." This constant stream of language, tied to real-world objects and experiences, is far more powerful than any app. Reading books should be interactive—point to pictures, ask questions, and use different voices.

- **Play Games that Build the Brain's CEO.** Simple, classic games are powerful tools for building executive functions. "Simon Says" teaches listening and impulse control. "Red Light, Green Light" helps with response inhibition. Board games with simple rules teach turn-taking and focus. These activities are fun, relational, and more effective at building a child's prefrontal cortex than any "brain game" on a tablet.
- **Embrace Boredom.** It is in the moments *without* structured activity or stimulation that creativity and self-reliance are born. Resist the urge to fill every moment of your child's day with an activity or a screen. Allowing a child to be bored gives them the mental space to listen to their own thoughts, invent their own games, and discover their own interests. If your child says, "I'm bored," use it as an opportunity to show them that boredom can be a valuable space—one that invites imagination and sparks creativity.

Key Neuroscience Concepts

- *Executive Functions:* A set of crucial brain skills housed in the prefrontal cortex, including impulse control, working memory, and cognitive flexibility. These skills are built through real-world interactive play, not passive screen consumption.
- *Joint Attention:* The shared focus of two individuals on the same object or event while being aware of each other's focus. This is a fundamental building block for language development and is absent during solo screen time.
- *Language Development Delay:* Research indicates a strong correlation between excessive screen time in toddlers and delays in expressive language, as screens cannot replicate the rich reciprocal "serve and return" dance of human conversation.

Key Psychoanalytic Concepts

- *Imaginative Play as Work:* From a psychoanalytic perspective, a child's pretend play is not frivolous. It is the essential "work" of processing complex emotions, developing creativity, resolving internal conflicts, and building a robust sense of self.
- *The "Inner World":* The concept of a rich internal landscape of thoughts, memories, and imagination. This inner world is cultivated during periods of unstructured time and even boredom, which are often crowded out by constant external stimulation from screens.
- *Language as Relational:* Language is more than vocabulary; it is the primary medium for connection. It is learned within the context of a relationship, and its development is dependent on the quality of that relational bond.

Chapter 2 References

Birken, C. S., et al. (2017). Handheld screen time linked with expressive language delay in infants. *Paediatrics & Child Health Conference*.

Key Neuroscience Concepts

Madigan, S., Browne, D., Racine, N., Mori, C., & Tough, S. (2019). Association Between Screen Time and Children's Performance on a Developmental Screening Test. *JAMA Pediatrics, 173*(3), 244–250.

University of Bath. (2021, January 26). Toddlers who use touchscreens may be more distractible. *ScienceDaily*. Retrieved from www.sciencedaily.com/releases/2021/01/210126082718.htm

3

When the Interpreter Is Preoccupied

The Psychoanalytic Impact of Technoference

The face of a parent is the first mirror in which a child discovers the self. In that responsive gaze, a child's feelings are reflected, named, and given meaning. This concept, described so elegantly by psychoanalyst D.W. Winnicott, is not mere poetry. It is the neurological and psychological mechanism by which a human mind begins to form. But what happens to the developing self when that mirror is cracked, or worse, perpetually turned away, reflecting instead the flat, cold light of a digital screen?

A growing child of five to eight is hungry for parental engagement. They want to share their successes, seek guidance with their challenges, and above all, feel truly listened to. Yet this natural desire collides with the reality of technoference, the constant interruption of in-person interactions by technology.

Technoference represents a direct assault on the quality of the caregiver-child relationship, creating repeated ruptures in connection and undermining the essential relational functions that allow the child to build trust, stability, and a coherent sense of self. From a psychoanalytic perspective, this relationship is the very foundation of development, now placed in jeopardy by the intrusion of screens.

The Broken Mirror and the Leaky Container

As discussed, Winnicott's concept of the face as a mirror is crucial. Similarly, Heinz Kohut emphasized the role of "mirroring self-object experiences," in which a caregiver's affirmation of a child's vitality helps build a cohesive sense of self. Parental absorption in screens fundamentally obstructs this vital function. The parent's gaze is directed at the screen, their facial expressions reflecting digital content rather than the child's inner world. When an infant looks to the parent—the primary source of social and emotional information—and finds them blank or focused elsewhere, the infant does not receive the necessary reflection of their own being. This can lead to a profound internalized experience of being unseen, which can impede healthy development and the capacity to regulate emotions.

Beyond mirroring, the caregiver serves another critical function, which Wilfred Bion (1962) termed "containment." He theorized that infants experience raw, overwhelming emotional states— "beta-elements"—that they cannot process. They psychically "project" this distress onto the caregiver, who, using their mature mind, metabolizes the anxiety and returns it to the infant in a more tolerable, thinkable form—"alpha-function." A screaming infant who is held and soothed is experiencing containment. This process is how a child learns, over time, to soothe themselves.

A parent distracted by a device becomes a "leaky container." Their attention is divided, their patience is thin, and their capacity for attunement is compromised. A study of caregivers conducted in fast-food restaurants, for instance, found a direct link between parents' absorption in their devices and a tendency to respond more harshly to their children's behavior (Radesky et al., 2014). An irritable or unavailable parent cannot effectively contain a child's distress. The anxiety is, in effect, handed right back to the child, leaving them overwhelmed and destabilized. This pattern, repeated over time, can lead to the development of maladaptive coping strategies and a diminished capacity for emotional resilience.

The Anxious Attachment to the Present-Absent Parent

Attachment theory, as developed by Bowlby and Ainsworth, posits that a child needs a secure base from which to explore the world. Technoference corrodes this base. The parent becomes a confusing "present-but-absent" object—physically in the room but emotionally unavailable. This is profoundly unsettling for a child. This inconsistency, where a parent is sometimes available and sometimes not, can foster an anxious attachment style wherein the child is always vigilant and uncertain about the caregiver's reliability.

The child learns that they must compete with the device for attention. This is not just a fleeting frustration; it can shape the child's internal object relations—their internalized template for how relationships work. The child may internalize a dynamic where they are in a painful triangular relationship: self–parent–device. In this internal world, the device can become a powerful rival, evoking feelings of jealousy, devaluation, and impotence that can carry forward into future relationships.

What Can Be Done?

Breaking the anxious triangle and restoring the primacy of the parent-child dyad requires conscious, deliberate action.

- **Restore the Dyad**. Intentionally create moments where the "third" is banished. This means putting the phone not just face down, but in another room entirely during key relational times such as during play, meals, and bedtime. This physically restores the two-person dynamic and sends a powerful message to the child (and to your own brain) that this relationship is the priority.
- **Narrate Your Use.** If you must use your phone in front of your child, narrate it. "I am looking up directions to the park," or "I am texting Daddy to see when he'll be home." This demystifies the

device, framing it as a simple tool you control rather than a magical object that controls you. It pulls the device out of the role of a mysterious rival and into the shared reality of the dyad.

- **Turn Your Body.** When your child speaks to you while you're on your phone, make a conscious effort to stop, turn your entire body toward them, make eye contact, and listen. This small physical act communicates a massive psychological shift: *You are more important than what I was just doing.* It actively breaks the triangle and prioritizes the human connection.

- **Embrace the Intensity.** Recognize that the urge to escape into a device is often a sign that the intensity of parenting is high. Instead of reaching for the phone, try reaching for your child. A hug, a moment of deep breathing together, or simply acknowledging the difficulty ("Wow, you have so much big energy right now!") can be a more effective and connecting way to manage the moment than disappearing into a screen.

Key Neuroscience Concepts

- *Still-Face Paradigm:* Infants show immediate distress when caregivers become unresponsive. Parents on phones re-create these moments throughout the day.
- *Competitive Attention:* The brain has limited attentional resources. A parent's brain is often forced into a direct competition between the needs of their child and the highly stimulating, dopamine-rewarding nature of a smartphone, which is engineered to win that battle.
- *Reward System Hijacking (Parental):* For a stressed and exhausted parent, the quick, predictable dopamine hit from a social media "like" or a game level-up can be more immediately rewarding than the slower, more demanding work of attuned childcare, leading to an unconscious but powerful pull toward the device.

Key Psychoanalytic Concepts

- *Technoference:* The disruption of face-to-face interaction by technology.
- *The Dyad:* The foundational two-person psychological unit, typically mother and infant, within which the primary sense of self is formed.
- *The "New Third":* The concept that the smartphone or digital device has intruded upon the sacred parent-child dyad, acting as a pathological "third object" in the room that disrupts the primary relationship.
- *The Device as Rival:* The child's unconscious perception of the device as a rival for the parent's love and attention. This can lead to feelings of jealousy, narcissistic injury (the feeling of not being the most important), and the internalization of a problematic relational triangle.

Chapter 3 References

Bion, W. R. (1962). A theory of thinking. *International Journal of Psycho-Analysis, 43*, 306–310.

McDaniel, B. T., & Radesky, J. S. (2018). Technoference: Parent distraction with technology and associations with child behavior problems. *Child Development, 89*(1), 100–109.

Prinz, W. (2012). *Open minds: The social making of agency and intentionality*. MIT Press.

Radesky, J. S., Kistin, C. J., Zuckerman, B., Nitzberg, K., Gross, J., Kaplan-Sanoff, M., Augustyn, M., & Silverstein, M. (2014). Patterns of mobile device use by caregivers and children during meals in fast food restaurants. *Pediatrics, 133*(4), e843–e849.

Kohut, H. (1971). *The analysis of the self: A systematic approach to the psychoanalytic treatment of narcissistic personality disorders*. University of Chicago Press.

McDaniel, B. T., & Radesky, J. S. (2018). Technoference: Parent distraction with technology and associations with child behavior problems. *Child Development, 89*(1), 100–109.

Turkle, S. (2011). *Alone together: Why we expect more from technology and less from each other*. Basic Books.

Tomopoulos, S., Dreyer, B. P., Berkule, S., Fierman, A. H., Brockmeyer, C., & Mendelsohn, A. L. (2010). Infant media exposure and toddler development. *Archives of Pediatrics & Adolescent Medicine, 164*(12), 1105–1111.

Winnicott, D. W. (1971). *Playing and reality*. Tavistock Publications. (Note: This is a more standard source for Winnicott's concept of the mother as a mirror).

Forging the Self Amid the Static

Trust, Autonomy, and the Path to Repair

The preceding chapters have detailed the myriad ways modern technology can invade the sacred space between parent and child. We have explored how the caregiver's distracted presence can fracture the mirroring process, create an unreliable "holding environment," and introduce the device as a powerful "new third" in the family dynamic. These are not trivial, momentary frustrations; they are systemic disruptions that strike at the very heart of how a human self is formed.

This chapter will now connect these digital-age phenomena to the foundational pillars of personality development as conceived by the pioneering psychoanalyst Erik Erikson. His theory of psychosocial development provides a powerful framework for understanding exactly what is at stake during a child's earliest years. When a parent's attention is consistently diverted by a screen, the issue is not merely one of rudeness or neglect. It is a direct threat to the successful resolution of the first three critical stages of life: the development of trust, the flourishing of autonomy, and the cultivation of initiative. The static of the digital world can, if we are not careful, drown out the signal of the developing self.

The Crisis of Trust

According to Erikson (1950), the first and most fundamental task of an infant is to resolve the crisis of *Trust vs. Mistrust*. In this stage, the infant asks a silent, existential question: *Is the world a safe, predictable, and loving place?* The answer is delivered not through words, but through the consistency and reliability of their caregiver. When the infant is hungry and is fed, cold and is warmed, distressed and is soothed, they build a foundational sense of trust. This trust in the caregiver becomes a template for trust in others, in the world, and ultimately, in oneself.

Technoference wages a direct war on this process. A parent perpetually distracted by a device provides, by definition, inconsistent and unpredictable care. The "present-but-absent" caregiver is profoundly confusing to an infant's nervous system. The baby may be held in their parent's arms yet feel emotionally abandoned. The parent's lap, which should be a secure base, becomes an unreliable landscape where attention can vanish without warning. This is the very essence of an environment that fosters mistrust. The infant learns that their needs are secondary to the demands of the glowing object, and the world begins to feel like a place where connection is precarious and unreliable. Research has consistently shown that parental sensitivity and responsiveness are the key ingredients of secure attachment; the chronic disruption of these qualities by technology logically paves the way for a deep-seated mistrust to take root (McDaniel & Radesky, 2018).

The Threat to Autonomy

Having hopefully established a foundation of trust, the toddler, from about 18 months to three years, embarks on the next great adventure: resolving the crisis of *Autonomy vs. Shame and Doubt*. This is the stage of "Me do it!" The toddler's core mission is to develop a sense of personal control over their physical skills and a sense of independence. They want to pour their own juice (and spill it), put on their own shoes (on the wrong feet), and explore every corner of their environment. The caregiver's role is to encourage these efforts and provide a safe boundary for exploration, allowing for mastery without excessive criticism.

A distracted caregiver is a poor supervisor for this delicate dance. The patience required to watch a toddler struggle for five minutes to put on a coat is immense; a parent seeking the quick dopamine hit of their social media feed may find this process intolerably slow and simply take over, robbing the child of a chance to succeed on their own. When a child's messy but enthusiastic attempts at self-feeding are met with an irritable sigh from a parent trying to read an email, the child doesn't learn to be neater; they learn a sense of shame about their efforts and doubt in their abilities. The parent who is looking at a screen cannot provide the watchful presence needed to be a "secure base" for exploration, potentially making the child more anxious and less adventurous.

The Stifling of Initiative

From roughly age three to five, the child enters the stage of *Initiative vs. Guilt.* Their world explodes with imagination, purpose, and planning. They don't just play; they create elaborate worlds, direct complex social dramas with their toys, and ask endless questions about how the world works. This is the stage of making, doing, and creating. When caregivers encourage this burgeoning initiative—by engaging in the pretend play, answering questions, and celebrating creations—the child develops a sense of purpose and confidence.

When a child's enthusiastic bid for engagement—"Daddy, watch this! Look what I built!"—is met with a distracted "Mmm-hmm, that's nice" from a parent looking at a screen, something vital is crushed. The child's initiative is dismissed. Repeatedly having their creative and social impulses rebuffed teaches them a painful lesson: their ideas are not important, and their desire to engage is an interruption. This can foster a pervasive sense of guilt, leading to a child who is passive, less likely to lead, and hesitant to trust their own creative impulses. They learn that it is better not to initiate than to risk the sting of being ignored.

The Principle of Relational Repair

The picture painted here is stark, yet the story does not end with damage. The human relationship, in its incredible resilience, has a built-in antidote: the capacity for repair. The goal of parenting is not to be a perfect, flawlessly attuned presence at all times—an impossible and perhaps even undesirable standard. Rather, the goal is to be a "good-enough" parent who, upon realizing a disconnection has occurred, has the capacity to mend it.

From a psychoanalytic view, repair is a profound act of containment. When a parent recognizes they were distracted and says, "I'm sorry, I was looking at my phone and wasn't listening. I can see you're frustrated with me. Let's try again," they are doing more than apologizing. They are "containing" the child's legitimate frustration, acknowledging its validity, and demonstrating that the relationship is strong enough to withstand negative moments and be restored. This act of mending the bond is what teaches a child that conflict is survivable and that connection can be regained, a cornerstone of lifelong relational health (Fonagy & Target, 2007).

From a neuroscience perspective, repair is an act of co-regulating a dysregulated nervous system. An ignored or dismissed child is a stressed child, flooded with cortisol. The act of repair—making eye contact, using a soothing tone, offering an apology and physical comfort—calms this stress response. It demonstrates to the child's brain, in a direct, biological way, that the relational environment has returned to a state of safety. Over time, repeated experiences of rupture followed by repair build a resilient brain, one that is wired for the optimistic belief that even when things go wrong, they can be made right again.

While the digital world presents a constant threat to the developing self, the power to build trust, foster autonomy, and encourage initiative still resides where it always has: in the parent's conscious, loving, and, when necessary, reparative presence.

What Can Be Done?

Supporting the child's early psychosocial development means protecting trust, encouraging autonomy, nurturing initiative, and modeling repair when disconnection occurs.

- **Protect Sacred Routines.** Make feeding, bedtime, and story time completely screen-free. These are the moments that form the foundation of trust, teaching a child that care is consistent and reliable.
- **Encourage Autonomy.** Let toddlers try—even if it means spills or shoes on the wrong feet. Patiently allowing them to practice self-care tasks fosters independence and a belief in their own competence.
- **Validate Initiative.** When a child says, "Watch this!" or invites you into imaginative play, give your full attention. Eye contact and presence communicate that their creativity matters and their ideas have value.
- **Repair the Rupture.** When distraction happens, acknowledge it and reconnect: "I'm sorry, I wasn't paying attention. I want to hear you now." This models resilience, teaches that conflict can be repaired, and restores trust.
- **Use Transitional Pauses.** Before re-engaging after checking a device, take a breath, set the phone aside fully, and turn toward your child. This signals clearly that your attention is back where it belongs.
- **Model Mindful Device Use.** When you must use a device, explain why: "I'm checking directions for us." This reframes the phone as a tool, not a rival, and reassures your child that their needs remain primary.

Key Neuroscience Concepts

- *Neural Pathways of Trust:* The neurological concept that consistent, responsive care builds strong, predictable neural pathways for security in an infant's brain. Inconsistent care, often caused by technoference, can create disorganized, anxious neural pathways.
- *The Neurobiology of Mastery:* The process by which a toddler's successful efforts at exploring and mastering their environment (e.g., learning to walk, stacking blocks) strengthens crucial connections in their motor cortex and prefrontal cortex, a process that requires a safe environment provided by an attentive caregiver.
- *Co-Regulation of the Nervous System:* The biological reality that a calm caregiver can soothe a distressed child's nervous system through physical touch and a soothing voice, lowering stress hormones like cortisol. Relational repair after a rupture is a key example of this process in action.

Key Psychoanalytic Concepts

- *Autonomy vs. Shame and Doubt (Erikson):* The second psychosocial crisis, during which a toddler strives for independence. This is supported by a patient caregiver but thwarted by an impatient or distracted one, leading to the toddler feeling shame about their capabilities.
- *Initiative vs. Guilt (Erikson):* The third psychosocial crisis, during which a preschooler's drive to create, plan, and initiate play must be encouraged. If their bids for engagement are consistently ignored, they can develop a pervasive sense of guilt about their own impulses.
- *The Principle of Relational Repair:* The crucial idea that the act of mending a disconnection between parent and child is more important for long-term psychological health than being a "perfect" parent. Repair teaches the child that relationships are resilient and that connection can be restored after a rupture.

Chapter 4 References

Erikson, E. H. (1950). *Childhood and society*. W. W. Norton & Company.

Fonagy, P., & Target, M. (2007). The rooting of the mind in the body: New links between attachment theory and psychoanalysis. *Journal of the American Psychoanalytic Association, 55*(2), 411–456.

McDaniel, B. T., & Radesky, J. S. (2018). Technoference: Parent distraction with technology and associations with child behavior problems. *Child Development, 89*(1), 100–109.

Tronick, E., & Beeghly, M. (2011). Infants' meaning-making and the development of mental health problems. *American Psychologist, 66*(2), 107–119. (Note: This work builds on the "still-face" paradigm, which is highly relevant to the concept of repair after disconnection.)

Winnicott, D. W. (1964). *The child, the family, and the outside world*. Penguin Books.

PART 2

The Tween and Adolescent Years (8–18)

5

The Adolescent Brain on Screens

A Tale of Two Systems

The brain of a tween or adolescent is one of nature's most magnificent and volatile construction sites. It is not a finished product, nor is it simply a smaller version of an adult brain. It is a system undergoing a radical time-delayed overhaul. Understanding this process is key to understanding why the digital world, with its endless rewards and social pressures, holds such powerful and often perilous sway over young people.

This neurological story can be understood as a tale of two systems. The first is the limbic system, the brain's ancient and powerful hub for emotion, pleasure, and threat detection. It is the engine of our most primal drives: the thrill of novelty, the warmth of social acceptance, the sting of rejection. In adolescents this system is fully developed and firing on all cylinders, supercharged by the hormonal surges of puberty. It is the brain's gas pedal, pressed firmly to the floor.

The second system is the prefrontal cortex, the brain's CEO. As discussed earlier, the PFC governs executive functions such as impulse control, long-term planning, and weighing future consequences. It is the brain's brakes. Crucially, the PFC is the last part of the brain to be fully myelinated and mature, a process that is not complete until the mid-twenties (Giedd et al., 1999).

The result is a brain fundamentally imbalanced: a high-octane emotional engine with unreliable brakes. This mismatch explains much of classic adolescent behavior, from risk-taking to intense focus on peers to emotional volatility. Into this neurologically vulnerable state we have introduced the most potent "super-stimulus" ever invented: the smartphone.

The Hijacking of the Reward System

Social media platforms are not neutral tools. They are sophisticated reward-delivery systems engineered to exploit the brain's pleasure circuits. Every "like," comment, and notification triggers a small release of dopamine, the same neurotransmitter involved in eating, gambling, and substance use (Sherman et al., 2016). For the adolescent brain with its fully developed limbic system primed for reward, this creates a powerful and potentially addictive feedback loop.

The anticipation of a social reward—checking to see who "liked" a photo—can become more compelling than real-world activities. This cycle of craving and gratification leads to compulsive use as the brain learns to chase the next small hit of validation. The variable reward schedule of social media, in which notifications arrive unpredictably, is notoriously effective at reinforcing this behavior, mirroring the mechanics of a slot machine.

The Social Brain Under Digital Stress

The adolescent brain is exquisitely tuned to social information. Neuroimaging studies show that the mere presence of peers alters how adolescents process information and make decisions. This social sensitivity is adaptive, designed to help young people navigate the crucial task of finding their place in a group. Social media, however, exposes this delicate system to unprecedented stress.

Instead of a manageable circle of friends, an adolescent now faces a vast, curated, and competitive global arena. The amygdala, which processes emotional cues and threats, is bombarded with ambiguous information. Is a friend's photo, taken at a party the reader of the post wasn't invited to, a deliberate snub or an oversight? Does a lack of "likes" on a post signify rejection? The adolescent brain responds to these digital cues with the same intensity as it would in-person encounters (Crone & Konijn, 2018). The result is a chronic state of social vigilance, comparison, and fear of missing out (FOMO) that drains the developing brain and amplifies anxiety.

The Erosion of Sleep

Sleep is not a luxury. It is a critical biological function, especially for the adolescent brain, which undergoes massive nighttime reorganization during these years. Sleep consolidates memories and strengthens neural pathways. Without it, the brain struggles to regulate mood, attention, and learning.

Screens sabotage adolescent sleep in two primary ways. First is the physiological impact of blue light, which suppresses melatonin, the hormone that signals the body to wind down. Second, and often more disruptive, is the emotional activation of screen content. Socially charged interactions late at night keep the limbic system in a state of high alert. A teenager may be physically in bed, but their brain is emotionally at a party, replaying conversations or stewing over a perceived slight. This state of hyperarousal is the enemy of restorative sleep, leaving adolescents chronically deprived and cognitively compromised.

What Can Be Done?

Helping a teen navigate this period is not about banning technology, but about supporting their brain's development and helping them build the skills to manage the digital world wisely.

- **Build the Brakes.** The best way to counteract an overactive gas pedal is to strengthen the brakes. Encourage activities that build the prefrontal cortex. This includes long-term projects with delayed gratification (learning an instrument, training for a 5K race, building something complex), mindfulness practices that strengthen attention, and real-world problem-solving.

- **Prioritize Sleep Hygiene.** The bedroom must be a screen-free sanctuary. Enforce a family rule that all devices are charged overnight in a central location, such as the kitchen. This is often the most resisted rule, and the most important one. Encourage a "digital sunset" an hour before bed during which screens are replaced with books, quiet music, or conversation.

- **Talk About the "Why."** Explain the "gas pedal and brakes" model to your teen. When they understand the neuroscience behind their own impulses, it can be empowering. It externalizes the problem, framing it not as a personal failing (*I have no self-control*) but as a predictable brain state that they can learn to manage.

- **Encourage Offline Connection.** The only effective antidote to the shallow validation of online "likes" is the deep satisfaction of real-world connection. Actively support and facilitate face-to-face time with friends. Make your home a welcoming place for your teen's social circle to gather.

Key Neuroscience Concepts

- *Limbic System vs. Prefrontal Cortex (PFC):* The core neurological mismatch of adolescence. The limbic system (the brain's emotional, pleasure-seeking "gas pedal") is fully developed and highly active, while the PFC (the rational, impulse-controlling "brakes") is not yet mature. This imbalance makes teens uniquely susceptible to the rewards of social media and risk-taking behavior.

- *Dopamine Reward Loop:* Social media platforms are engineered to trigger the release of dopamine, the brain's "feel-good" neurotransmitter, through unpredictable rewards such as "likes" and notifications. This creates a powerful, potentially addictive feedback loop that can lead to compulsive use.

- *Sleep Disruption:* The blue light from screens suppresses melatonin production, disrupting the sleep cycle. Further, late-night social engagement activates the emotional centers of the brain, making restorative sleep—which is critical for memory consolidation and brain development—physiologically difficult.

Key Psychoanalytic Concepts

- *Primal Drives and Social Needs:* The adolescent's behavior is driven by powerful, primal needs for social acceptance, peer validation, and novelty. Social media offers a "super-stimulus" that directly and powerfully targets these fundamental drives.
- *Risk-Taking as Developmental:* A certain amount of risk-taking is a normal and necessary part of adolescent development, as it helps the teen separate from parents and form their own identity. However, the digital world presents new, less visible, and often more dangerous forms of risk.
- *Fear of Missing Out (FOMO):* Not just a cultural slang term but a genuine psychological anxiety rooted in the deep-seated adolescent need for belonging. This fear is a primary driver of compulsive online engagement.

Chapter 5 References

Crone, E. A., & Konijn, E. A. (2018). Media use and brain development during adolescence. *Nature Communications, 9*(1), 588.

Giedd, J. N., Blumenthal, J., Jeffries, N. O., Castellanos, F. X., Liu, H., Zijdenbos, A., Paus, T., Evans, A.C., & Rapoport, J. L. (1999). Brain development during childhood and adolescence: a longitudinal MRI study. *Nature Neuroscience, 2*(10), 861–863.

Sherman, L. E., Payton, A. A., Hernandez, L. M., Greenfield, P. M., & Dapretto, M. (2016). The power of the like in adolescence: Effects of peer influence on neural and behavioral responses to social media. *Psychological Science, 27*(7), 1027–1035.

6

The Search for Self

Identity, Social Mirrors, and the Digital Maze

If the adolescent brain is a construction site, the primary project being built is a coherent sense of self. According to Erik Erikson, the central psychosocial crisis of the teenage years is identity versus role confusion. The fundamental question of this life stage is *Who am I?* To answer it, adolescents must explore different roles, values, beliefs, and relationships. They experiment with personas, affiliate with groups, and test out ways of being in the world.

Successful navigation of this stage leads to a stable sense of personal identity. Failure to do so can result in confusion, fragility, and an unstable sense of self. This critical process of identity formation does not happen in isolation. It unfolds in a social context; we discover who we are by seeing ourselves reflected in the eyes of others. This "social mirror" is composed of interactions with family, the feedback of teachers and mentors, and—most powerfully during adolescence—the acceptance or rejection of peers.

The Distorted Mirror of Social Media

For all of human history until roughly 15 years ago, the social mirror, while sometimes harsh, was at least real. It was made up of face-to-face interactions with a finite number of people. It included nonverbal cues, shared experiences, and the complex data of embodied human presence.

Social media has replaced this real mirror with a distorted digital one. The "reflection" a teen encounters online is rarely authentic. It is curated, filtered, and performance-based.

Adolescents find themselves comparing their messy private realities—their insecurities, arguments at home, "bad hair" days—with the polished highlight reels of others.

This distortion fuels social comparison, which research strongly links to depression and low self-esteem in adolescents (Vogel et al., 2014). The ego ideal—an adolescent's internal image of who they should be—is no longer built from observing real, flawed, but admirable figures in their community. Instead, it is shaped by the impossible standards of influencers and online peers. The result is often a painful conviction that one's authentic self is fundamentally inadequate.

From a neuroscientific perspective, this matters because the adolescent brain is exceptionally plastic. The reward system is primed for social validation, and each "like" or comment provides a dopamine surge. When identity formation is anchored in these distorted cues, the brain's wiring begins to favor external approval over internal coherence. In other words, the adolescent is not just psychologically vulnerable to comparison; their neural pathways are literally being tuned to seek it.

The Erosion of Real-World Relational Skills

Building a stable identity requires more than introspection. It requires practicing social competence in real time. The ability to read subtle nonverbal cues, navigate group dynamics, and show empathy emerges from thousands of embodied encounters. A friend's shift in tone, the shared glance of teammates, or the act of comforting someone in distress all serve as lessons in how to be human.

When large portions of social life migrate online, the development of these skills can stall. Digital communication strips away tone, facial expression, and body language, leaving gaps that adolescents fill with assumptions. Misunderstandings proliferate, and social drama intensifies.

Empathy is harder to cultivate when a teen is shielded from the immediate impact of their words on another person's face. Over time, reliance on digital interaction can leave adolescents less able to manage nuance and ambiguity in relationships.

Neuroscience underscores this point. The mirror neuron system, which fires both when we act and when we observe someone else's action, plays a central role in empathy and social learning. Without frequent embodied interaction, this system atrophies. Functional MRI studies show that adolescents heavily engaged in digital communication exhibit weaker activation in brain regions linked to social cognition. In short, the less we practice reading faces, the less skilled our brains become at it.

The Illusion of Connection

Adolescence is also a critical period for learning how to manage intense emotions and develop healthy defenses. Everyone uses defenses to protect against anxiety. Mature ones include humor, sublimation (channeling difficult feelings into creative work), or seeking support.

Digital life often fosters less adaptive defenses. A socially anxious teen may retreat into the online world instead of confronting their fear in person. A conflict may be resolved by "ghosting," a form of denial and avoidance. Most pervasively, online culture encourages projective identification, in which unacceptable feelings are projected onto others. Stripped of context, the online other becomes a lightening rod for our own disavowed parts. The troll we attack may in fact be a shadow of ourselves. This dynamic arrests the growth of self-awareness and emotional regulation.

Neuroscience again shows a parallel process. Chronic digital overengagement activates the amygdala, the brain's threat detector, while underengaging the prefrontal cortex regions needed for reflection and regulation. In practical terms, the adolescent brain becomes wired for vigilance and reaction rather than for thoughtful processing. What psychoanalysis describes as a collapse into projection neuroscience describes as an imbalance between limbic hyperactivity and underdeveloped regulatory systems. Both perspectives reveal the same outcome: a fragile, externally driven self that struggles to develop.

What Can Be Done?

Guiding a teen through the digital maze is about fostering critical thinking and building a robust internal sense of self that is not dependent on external digital validation.

- **Encourage an "Identity Portfolio."** Identity is built from real-world competence and contribution. Encourage your teen to assemble a "portfolio" of experiences that are offline and character-building. This could include a part-time job, volunteering, joining a club or team, mastering a hobby, or becoming involved in a community or faith group. These activities provide a sense of purpose and self-worth that "likes" cannot replicate.
- **Become a Media Literacy Mentor.** Talk openly and nonjudgmentally about the nature of social media. Ask critical questions such as "Why do you think she only posts photos where she looks perfect?" and "What is the business model of this app? What are they selling?" Open up discussions with statements like "Let's talk about the difference between someone's online performance and their real life." This teaches them to be critical consumers of media rather than passive believers.
- **Prioritize Face-to-Face Time.** Insist on device-free family dinners. Actively support and facilitate in-person hangouts with their friends. When you talk with your teen, ask them to put their phone away

and give them your full, undivided attention. This models the value you place on genuine uninterrupted connection.

- **Cultivate Empathy.** Empathy is a skill that requires practice. Watch movies or read books together and talk about the characters' motivations and feelings. Discuss real-world ethical dilemmas. Engage them in community service where they can interact with people from different walks of life. These activities build the "empathy muscle" in ways that scrolling through a feed cannot.

Key Neuroscience Concepts

- *The Social Brain Network:* A network of brain regions, including the medial prefrontal cortex and superior temporal sulcus, that is specialized in deciphering the thoughts, feelings, and intentions of others. This network is highly active during adolescence and requires rich, real-world social data to develop properly.
- *Nonverbal Cue Processing:* A significant portion of human communication is nonverbal. The brain is exquisitely tuned to interpret facial expressions, tone of voice, and body language. Overreliance on text-based digital communication can starve the brain of this essential data, potentially stunting the development of social perception skills.

Key Psychoanalytic Concepts

- *Identity vs. Role Confusion (Erikson):* The central psychosocial crisis of adolescence. The primary task is to develop a coherent sense of self by exploring different roles, values, and beliefs. Social media can complicate this process by presenting a distorted, performance-based version of social reality.
- *The Social Mirror:* The concept that we discover who we are by seeing ourselves reflected in the eyes of others. Social media replaces the real-world social mirror with a distorted digital one, where teens compare their internal reality to the curated highlight reels of others, often leading to feelings of inadequacy.
- *The Ego-Ideal:* The internalized image of who one should be. In the digital age, this ideal is often formed not by observing real, flawed community members but by comparing oneself to the impossible standards of online influencers and filtered peers.

Chapter 6 References

Erikson, E. H. (1968). *Identity: Youth and crisis.* W. W. Norton & Company.

Vogel, E. A., Rose, J. P., Roberts, L. R., & Eckles, K. (2014). Social comparison, social media, and self-esteem. *Psychology of Popular Media Culture, 3*(4), 206–222.

7

The Vanishing Interior

Solitude, Self-Regulation, and the Adolescent Brain

In our clinical work with distressed adolescents, one of the most common and challenging issues we confront is a diminished capacity for self-regulation. Self-regulation is the ability to control and manage one's thoughts, emotions, and behaviors to adapt to changing circumstances. It is the bedrock of psychological maturity, allowing us to delay gratification, tolerate difficult feelings, and make considered choices. This crucial skill, however, is not innate; it is built over time, and one of its most important ingredients is the ability to be alone.

The Lost Art of Solitude

For centuries, thinkers have understood that solitude is not the same as loneliness. Loneliness is a painful lack of connection, whereas solitude is the constructive, voluntary state of being alone with one's own thoughts. It is in the quiet space of solitude that we develop an interior life. We untangle our feelings, engage in creative thought, process grief, and form a coherent sense of self. The psychoanalyst D.W. Winnicott (1958) called this "the capacity to be alone," arguing that it is a hallmark of emotional maturity developed in early childhood through the experience of being alone in the presence of a nonintrusive caregiver.

In the age of the smartphone, true solitude is becoming a lost art. Silence has become intolerable for many adolescents, and any moment of downtime is immediately filled by the stimulus of a screen. The human brain, which evolved to process external threats and opportunities, is often poorly trained to interpret and cope with internal data. Without the practice of being alone, silent, or even simply bored, the internal world can feel like a threatening place, generating an anxiety that can only be soothed by external distraction.

The Digital Intrusion and the Fear of Missing Out

We now have a generation of young people who have been in a near-perpetual state of stimulation since childhood. They feel a powerful need to be constantly connected to avoid being left out. This anxiety has been given its own acronym, FOMO, from "fear of missing out." First identified in the early 2000s, FOMO is the apprehension that one might miss out on rewarding experiences that others are having, and it is a powerful driver of compulsive social media use (Przybylski et al., 2013).

The perceived need for this constant electronic connection prevents adolescents from engaging in the vital developmental task of learning to be with themselves. Instead of turning inward to self-soothe or problem-solve, they turn outward to the endless scroll of a feed. Their emotions are not processed, but rather outsourced to the distraction of a screen.

The Neurological Cost: The Addicted Brain

This cycle of anxiety and distraction has a clear neurological correlate. When an adolescent relies on screens to manage their emotions, they are engaging in a form of behavioral addiction. The withdrawal from screens is as real as withdrawal from some substances, often leading to cravings, irritability, explosive anger, and depression. Parents who have tried to enforce a "digital detox" know this reality intimately; the process is rarely peaceful.

Imaging studies help explain why. Excessive social media usage has been linked to changes in brain structure, including reductions in gray matter in areas like the amygdala. The amygdala is a key part of the brain's limbic system that appraises the emotional meaning of sensory input. An underdeveloped or dysregulated amygdala can impair a person's ability to interpret social cues and emotions correctly, hampering their ability to form deep, authentic relationships. This same neurological pattern—a highly reactive limbic system and a less-developed prefrontal cortex—is also a known risk factor for substance abuse and other risky behaviors. In this sense, social media use not only provides a potential behavioral addiction but may also prime the brain for other dependencies.

What Can Be Done?

Helping an adolescent develop the capacity to be alone and to self-regulate is one of the greatest gifts a caregiver can provide. It is about nurturing their internal world so it becomes a safe and interesting place to be.

- **Schedule "Do Nothing" Time.** Just as you would schedule homework or sports, schedule quiet time with no devices. Start with just 10 to 15 minutes a day. This is not a punishment but an exercise. The goal is to allow the mind to wander, to be bored, and to see what thoughts or creative ideas emerge from the silence.
- **Promote Solitary Hobbies.** Encourage activities that require deep solitary focus. This could be drawing, learning an instrument, building models, coding, or writing. These hobbies are powerful because they teach a teen to find a state of "flow" and satisfaction that comes from within rather than from external validation.

- **Model Solitude.** Let your teen see you being comfortably alone. Let them see you reading a book, listening to music with your eyes closed, or simply sitting on the porch thinking. Narrate it ("I just need about 20 minutes of quiet time to recharge my brain."). This normalizes solitude and frames it as a healthy restorative practice.
- **Introduce Journaling.** Journaling is a structured way to engage in self-reflection. It provides a private space for a teen to untangle their thoughts and feelings without judgment. Provide them with a simple notebook and pen, with no pressure to share what they write. It is a tool for building self-awareness, the first step in self-regulation.

Key Neuroscience Concepts

- *Amygdala Regulation:* Excessive screen use and the associated stress and anxiety have been linked to changes in the amygdala. A dysregulated amygdala can impair the ability to accurately interpret emotional threats and social cues, and is a known risk factor for anxiety disorders and addiction.
- *The "Default Mode Network" (DMN):* A network of brain regions that is active when the mind is at rest and not focused on an external task. This network is associated with self-reflection, daydreaming, and creative thought. Constant external stimulation from screens can suppress the DMN, inhibiting the development of a rich inner world.

Key Psychoanalytic Concepts

- *The Capacity to Be Alone (Winnicott):* A hallmark of emotional maturity, defined as the ability to be alone with oneself in a comfortable, constructive way. This capacity is developed, not innate, and is threatened by an environment that makes silence and downtime feel intolerable.
- *Self-Regulation:* The ability to manage one's own internal states—thoughts, emotions, and impulses. This skill is built through the practice of tolerating difficult feelings and developing internal coping strategies, a process that is often short-circuited when a screen is used as an immediate emotional escape.
- *Behavioral Addiction:* The concept that processes, not just substances, can become addictive. The cycle of craving, compulsive use, and withdrawal experienced by many teens with their devices shares core neurological and psychological features with substance addiction.

Chapter 7 References

Long, C. R., & Averill, J. R. (2003). Solitude: An exploration of benefits of being alone. *Journal for the Theory of Social Behaviour, 33*(1), 21–44.

Przybylski, A. K., Murayama, K., DeHaan, C. R., & Gladwell, V. (2013). Motivational, emotional, and behavioral correlates of fear of missing out. *Computers in Human Behavior, 29*(4), 1841–1848.

Winnicott, D. W. (1958). The capacity to be alone. *International Journal of Psycho-Analysis, 39*, 416–420.

8

The Game of Thrones

Parents, Teens, and the Great Screen Battle

For parents of tweens and adolescents, screen time is a fact of life—and a source of near-constant tension. The daily struggles over "just five more minutes," the phone at the dinner table, or the homework put off in favor of a game are familiar to millions. These tensions are not merely a clash of wills; they represent a fundamental conflict between the developmental needs of the adolescent and the powerful, persuasive design of modern technology.

The Battlefield: The Parent vs. Persuasive Technology

When a parent tries to get their teen to log off, they are not just up against their child's impulses; they are up against some of the most brilliant and well-funded software engineers in the world. Apps, games, and social media platforms are built using principles of "persuasive technology" designed with the express purpose of capturing and holding our attention (Alter, 2017).

Features like endless scrolling, auto-playing videos, and variable reward notifications are engineered to keep users hooked. Online games often reward continuous play and even penalize players for abandoning a session, making it genuinely difficult for a teen to quit when called to dinner. A parent is not just asking their child to stop having fun; they are asking them to defy a system expertly designed to keep them hooked in. Framing the struggle in this way—as Parent and Child vs. The Algorithm—can be a more collaborative and less adversarial approach.

The Adolescent's Experience: Social Survival

From a teen's perspective, the request to "just get off" can feel like a request to stop breathing. Their social world lives on these platforms. Being offline is not just boring, it risks social irrelevance. There is immense pressure to keep up with the latest memes, to be included in the group chat, and to be present when their friends are online.

This social dynamic is a powerful force that parents often underestimate. For a teen, being told to log off in the middle of a multiplayer game is not simply an interruption; it is a public social failure in front of peers. The "fear of missing out" is not an abstraction; it is the concrete fear that friendships will evolve without them and inside jokes will be formed in their absence.

This puts them in a vicious trap, caught between the demands of their parents and the perceived demands of their social survival.

The Parent's Dilemma: The Challenge of Co-Regulation

Parents often feel underequipped to handle these new digital challenges. This is made worse by the fact that many parents are wrestling with their own screen-time habits. When a parent scrolls through Instagram while telling their child to read a book, the "Do as I say, not as I do" message is received loud and clear, and any parental authority on the subject is undermined.

Despite these challenges, parents remain the most powerful influence in a teen's life. The key is to shift from a model of control to one of connection and *co-regulation*. Co-regulation is the process by which parents and teens work together to manage emotions and solve problems. It involves acknowledging the teen's feelings, setting collaborative goals, and finding solutions together. Research shows that a strong parent-teen relationship, one in which the teen feels understood and respected, is a powerful protective factor against the risks of the digital world (Feldman, 2020). Even during adolescence, the secure attachment formed in early life continues to provide a "secure base" from which the teen can navigate new challenges.

What Can Be Done?

Moving from conflict to collaboration is the central task for families in the digital age. It requires communication, empathy, and clear, consistent boundaries.

- **Create a Family Tech Plan, Together.** Instead of imposing rules from on high, sit down as a family to create a written tech plan. Let your teen have a voice in the process. This document should cover things like tech-free times (dinner, one hour before bed), tech-free zones (bedrooms), and consequences for breaking the rules. When a teen helps create the plan, they have buy-in and are more likely to follow it.
- **Practice Co-Regulation, Not Control.** Instead of yelling, "Get off the game now!" try a co-regulating approach. Give a 15-minute warning. Then approach them calmly and say, "I see you're in the middle of something important to you. We agreed dinner is at 6:30. How can you start wrapping this up so you can join us?" This acknowledges their reality while holding the boundary.
- **Model the Behavior You Want to See.** This is the hardest part. Parents must lead by example. Announce your own intentions: "I'm putting my phone on the charger for the next hour so I can focus on our conversation." When you model this, you demonstrate that you too are capable of prioritizing connection over screens.

- **Use Their World as a Bridge.** Demonstrate genuine curiosity about their digital lives. Ask them to show you their favorite game or explain a TikTok trend. Co-viewing or co-playing, even for 20 minutes, can be a powerful point of connection. It shows them you respect their world and opens the door for conversations about the parts of it that worry you.

Key Neuroscience Concepts

- *Persuasive Technology:* The deliberate design of digital products to influence human behavior, often by exploiting psychological vulnerabilities. Features like infinite scroll and variable reward notifications are not accidental; they are engineered to capture and hold attention, making it difficult for an adolescent's still-developing PFC to disengage.
- *Cognitive Load:* The limited amount of information the brain can hold and process at one time. The constant demands of online games and social notifications create a high cognitive load, leaving fewer mental resources for important tasks like schoolwork or real-world problem-solving.

Key Psychoanalytic Concepts

- *Co-Regulation:* The process by which a caregiver helps a child or adolescent manage their emotional state. In adolescence, this evolves into a more collaborative process where parents and teens work together to set goals and solve problems, moving from a model of parental control to one of connection and mutual influence.
- *Modeling:* The powerful, often unconscious process by which children and teens absorb the behaviors and attitudes of their parents. A parent's own screen habits are a primary model for their teen's relationship with technology.
- *The Secure Base (Adolescence):* While the nature of the relationship changes, parents continue to serve as a secure base throughout adolescence. A teen who feels their parents are a reliable source of support and understanding is better equipped to navigate the risks and challenges of the outside world, including the digital one.

Chapter 8 References

Alter, A. (2017). *Irresistible: The rise of addictive technology and the business of keeping us hooked*. Penguin Press.

Feldman, R. (2020). The adaptive parent-child brain: The biological basis of parenting and its effects on child development. In *Parenting and child development* (pp. 25–50). Springer, Cham.

Maslow, A. H. (1943). A theory of human motivation. *Psychological Review, 50*(4), 370–396.

Twenge, J. M. (2017). *iGen: Why today's super-connected kids are growing up less rebellious, more tolerant, less happy—and completely unprepared for adulthood—and what that means for the rest of us*. Atria Books.

9

The Overwhelmed Ego

Anxiety and Depression in an Age of Overstimulation

The human brain is a masterpiece of evolution, honed over millennia to process external information, appraise it for survival value, and guide behavior. For our ancestors, the data sets were limited: Is that a predator? Is this fruit edible? Is this person a friend or foe? Today, the information load is a torrential flood.

The modern adolescent brain must navigate this flood with neurological equipment not designed for such intensity. Since the arrival of the smartphone, the brain has been subject to a relentless 24/7 assault of stimulation. Here, psychoanalytic theory provides a powerful lens.

Freud described the ego as the psyche's manager, mediating between the impulsive id and the moral constraints of the superego while simultaneously negotiating external reality. The ego's task is to cope, to regulate, and to maintain equilibrium.

When the ego is perpetually bombarded by notifications, social updates, news alerts, and digital demands, it becomes overwhelmed. Its ability to process reality, manage internal states, and regulate emotion falters. This erosion of ego capacity is not a minor inconvenience; it is a direct pathway to the mental health crises of anxiety and depression that dominate the lives of many adolescents today.

The Anxious Brain in an Always-On World

Anxiety, clinically, is more than worry. It is hypervigilance, physiological arousal, and the sense of impending threat without clear cause. The digital world functions as an anxiety-generating machine. Constant exposure to emotionally charged information—from tragic global events to perceived social slights on Instagram—keeps the adolescent nervous system in a state of chronic high alert.

This is intensified by what psychologists call the availability heuristic: the brain judges the importance of an event by how easily it comes to mind (Tversky & Kahneman, 1973). Catastrophic stories are more available, and the adolescent brain, still developing the capacity for perspective and regulation, struggles to contextualize them. The result is a sense that danger is everywhere and always imminent.

Neuroscience reinforces this picture. The amygdala, central to threat detection, becomes hyperactive under constant stimulation, while the underdeveloped prefrontal cortex lacks the regulatory maturity to restore calm. Prolonged hyperarousal triggers the body's stress system, flooding the bloodstream with cortisol. When a child is exposed to high levels of cortisol for long periods, it harms brain areas responsible for learning and attention. The hippocampus, which supports memory, becomes damaged, making it harder to remember things and increasing confusion. The prefrontal cortex, which helps with focus and self-control, also weakens, making it harder to concentrate. Meanwhile, the amygdala becomes overactive and starts misreading situations, leading the child to see the world as more threatening or confusing than it really is. What psychoanalysis describes as an ego under siege neuroscience captures as a dysregulated limbic-prefrontal circuit.

Layered on top is the relentless pressure of digital social life. The expectation to text back immediately, maintain Snapchat "streaks," or never miss an online moment creates low-grade but chronic anxiety.

With no downtime for the nervous system to reset, this state easily tips into clinical anxiety disorders.

The Depressed Brain and the Collapse of Coping

When the ego's attempts to manage the flood of stimulation repeatedly fail, the psyche may default to another strategy: shutting down. Depression can be understood as the consequence of a psychic collapse, a retreat into helplessness when the ego abandons the effort to cope. The adolescent who spends hours scrolling alone in their room is not necessarily enjoying themselves. They may be numbing despair, retreating from demands that feel impossible to meet, or anesthetizing a sense of inadequacy with the low-effort stimulation of a screen.

The neuroscience of depression echoes this description. Excessive digital stress dysregulates the default mode network (DMN), the system that governs self-reflection and autobiographical thought. Instead of integrating experiences into a coherent sense of self, the DMN becomes stuck in rumination and self-criticism. At the same time, reward circuitry in the striatum shows blunted responses, leaving the adolescent less able to feel pleasure in offline life. The link between social media use and adolescent depression is robust (Twenge, 2020).

Social comparison, cyberbullying, and the displacement of real-world connection amplify the collapse of coping. Most concerning, this psychic and neurological retreat can culminate in suicidality. Research consistently shows a correlation between high social media use and suicidal ideation, particularly among adolescent girls (Allen, 2022; Twenge et al., 2018). The social dynamics of "swarming", or sudden online ostracism, as Margaret Atwood (2017) noted, can produce psychological pain so intense it feels unendurable. At its most tragic, this represents the ultimate failure of the ego: the inability to bear reality at all.

What Can Be Done?

Strengthening an adolescent's ego functions is a proactive way to build their resilience against the pressures of the digital world. It is about helping them become an effective manager of their own mind.

- **Practice "Single-Tasking."** In a world that prizes multitasking, encourage the opposite. Promote activities that require sustained singular focus, such as reading a chapter of a book, completing a puzzle, or practicing mindfulness. This trains the prefrontal cortex—the neurological seat of the ego—to focus and resist distraction, strengthening its ability to manage competing demands.
- **Build a "Digital Literacy" Shield.** Teach your teen to be a critical consumer of information. Talk about the availability heuristic. Ask questions like, "This news story is scary, but how likely is it to affect our daily lives?" and "What is the business model of this website? Are they trying to inform you or just keep you clicking?" This strengthens the ego's reality-testing function.
- **Schedule a Digital "Sabbath."** The ego, like any manager, needs time off. Work with your teen to schedule a regular period—whether it's one evening a week or one full day a month—where the entire family puts all screens away. This allows the nervous system to reset and demonstrates that life is not only possible but enjoyable without constant stimulation.
- **Prioritize Sleep.** An exhausted ego cannot function effectively. Protect sleep by enforcing a nonnegotiable "no screens in the bedroom" rule for the entire family. A well-rested brain is a more resilient brain, better equipped to manage the stresses of the day.

Key Neuroscience Concepts

- *Information Overload:* A state of cognitive exhaustion whereby the prefrontal cortex receives more data than it can effectively process. This leads to a breakdown in decision-making, increased anxiety, and a tendency to either make impulsive choices or shut down completely.

- *The Availability Heuristic:* A mental shortcut by which the brain judges the likelihood of an event based on how easily examples come to mind. The ubiquity of sensationalized and emotionally charged content online places dramatic, negative events front and center, leading to a skewed sense of risk and heightened ambient anxiety.

- *Neurobiology of Stress:* Constant stimulation and social pressure keep the body's stress-response system chronically activated. This elevated level of cortisol can be toxic to the brain, particularly impairing the function of the hippocampus (memory) and the prefrontal cortex (regulation).

Key Psychoanalytic Concepts

- *The Ego:* The part of the psyche that functions as the "manager" or "executive." It is responsible for mediating between our impulsive desires (the id), our moral conscience (the superego), and the demands of external reality.

- *Failure of Ego Functions:* The central idea that the constant overstimulation of the digital world weakens the ego's ability to perform its essential duties of coping, regulating emotion, and testing reality. Clinical anxiety and depression can be understood as symptoms of this ego failure.

- *Psychic Retreat:* A defense mechanism by which, faced with an overwhelming reality, the psyche withdraws. An adolescent endlessly scrolling in their room may be in a state of psychic retreat, using the screen's low-effort stimulation to numb feelings of helplessness and psychic pain.

Chapter 9 References

Allen, C. (2022, November 17). *10-year BYU study shows elevated suicide risk from excess social media time for young teen girls.* BYU News.

Atwood, M. (2017, March 10). Margaret Atwood on what 'The Handmaid's Tale' means in the age of Trump. *The New York Times.*

Tversky, A., & Kahneman, D. (1973). Availability: A heuristic for judging frequency and probability. *Cognitive Psychology, 5*(2), 207–232.

Twenge, J. M. (2020). Why increases in adolescent depression and anxiety are not just a moral panic. *The Journal of the American Medical Association (JAMA) Pediatrics, 174*(6), 618–619.

Twenge, J. M., Joiner, T. E., Rogers, M. L., & Martin, G. N. (2018). Increases in depressive symptoms, suicide-related outcomes, and suicide rates among US adolescents after 2010 and links to increased new media screen time. *Clinical Psychological Science, 6*(1), 3–17.

.

10

The Shattered Mirror

How Screens Inhibit Empathy and Connection

Imagine watching a friend trip and fall. Before you even have a conscious thought, you likely flinch in sympathy. When a character in a movie weeps, you may feel a lump forming in your own throat. This profound human ability to feel *with* another person, to understand their intentions and share their emotional state, is the foundation of empathy and the glue of society. For decades, scientists have been uncovering the neurological basis for this ability: a remarkable class of brain cells known as mirror neurons.

The Brain's Empathy Engine

First discovered in monkeys and later identified in humans, mirror neurons are brain cells that fire both when we perform an action and when we observe someone else performing that same action (Rizzolatti & Craighero, 2004). When you reach for a cup, a specific set of neurons fires.

When you watch someone else reach for a cup, many of the same neurons fire as if you were performing the action yourself.

This system is, in effect, a built-in simulation machine. It allows us to understand the actions and intentions of others not by thinking, but by internally and unconsciously mirroring them. Neuroscientist V.S.

Ramachandran (2011) has called them "Gandhi neurons," arguing that they are the basis of empathy, effectively dissolving the barrier between self and other. This neural mirroring is believed to be fundamental to social learning, imitation, and our ability to feel compassion.

The Digital Disconnect

If the mirror neuron system is the engine of empathy, it requires high-quality fuel to run properly. That fuel is rich, real-time, face-to-face human interaction. The brain has been exquisitely tuned over millennia to process the complex synchronous data of a real-life encounter: the subtle shifts in facial expression, the nuanced tone of voice, the posture, the gestures. This is the data that our mirror neurons use to construct a rich internal model of another person's state of mind.

Much of today's digital communication starves the mirror neuron system of this essential data. A text message, a comment, or a curated social media post is stripped of nearly all the nonverbal cues that convey true emotional meaning. The brain simply does not have enough information to generate an accurate empathetic response. This can lead to a state of "empathy atrophy" in which the neural circuits for understanding others are underexercised and may become less efficient. An adolescent who spends the majority of their time communicating through text may be less skilled at interpreting the complex nonverbal signals of a classmate in distress or a parent's concern.

When the Mirror Reflects a Distortion

In addition to starving the empathy system, digital media hijacks the mimicry system. The same mirror neurons that allow for empathy also drive social contagion. Our brains are wired to imitate what we see, a trait that allowed for the rapid spread of culture and technology in human history. In the digital age, this can have dangerous consequences.

Viral "challenges," from harmless dances to life-threatening stunts, spread like wildfire precisely because our brains are built to mirror and imitate. The brain of an adolescent, with its underdeveloped prefrontal cortex, is particularly susceptible. It registers a behavior being performed by peers online and the impulse to mimic that behavior can be overwhelming, often overriding any rational assessment of risk. The normalization of once-unthinkable behaviors can occur rapidly when thousands of users are seen participating in them online, creating a distorted social reality where dangerous actions appear acceptable or even desirable.

What Can Be Done?

Cultivating empathy in the digital age requires a conscious effort to provide the brain with the rich real-world social data it needs to thrive.

- **Prioritize Embodied Interaction.** The single most effective way to build empathy is to ensure teens have consistent, meaningful face-to-face interaction. Encourage participation in team sports, drama clubs, and other group activities that require working together and reading each other's nonverbal cues in real time.
- **Use Media as an "Empathy Trainer."** Watch compelling films or read fiction with your teen and make it a practice to talk about the characters. Ask questions like, "Why do you think he did that?" "How do you think she felt when that happened?" and "What would you have done in that situation?" This uses media to actively practice perspective-taking.
- **Engage in Service.** Volunteering or engaging in community service is a powerful empathy-building experience. Interacting with people from different backgrounds, ages, and life circumstances expands a

teen's understanding of the world and connects them to a sense of shared humanity that goes beyond their own social bubble.

- **Discuss the "Why" Behind the Screen.** Talk to your teen about mirror neurons and social contagion. Explain that the urge to join a viral trend is a normal brain response, but that their prefrontal cortex has the power to question that impulse. Empowering them with this knowledge can help them move from being a passive mimic to a critical thinker.

Key Neuroscience Concepts

- *Mirror Neuron System:* A network of brain cells that fire both when we perform an action and when we observe that same action being performed by another. This system is considered the biological foundation for empathy, imitation, and our ability to understand the intentions of others.
- *"Empathy Atrophy":* The theory that an overreliance on text-based communication, which is stripped of nonverbal cues, can "starve" the mirror neuron system of the rich data it needs to develop. This may lead to a reduced capacity for deep, intuitive empathy.
- *Social Contagion:* The phenomenon of behaviors, emotions, and ideas spreading rapidly through a group. Our mirror neuron system's imitative function makes us highly susceptible to this phenomenon, which is why viral trends and challenges (both positive and negative) are so powerful online.

Key Psychoanalytic Concepts

- *Empathy:* The mature capacity to feel *with* another person. Psychoanalytic theory posits that empathy is not innate but is developed through thousands of embodied face-to-face interactions where one learns to read and respond to the subtle cues of another's internal state.
- *Identification and Mimicry:* The unconscious process of taking on the characteristics and behaviors of others. This is a cornerstone of learning and social development, but online it can be hijacked, leading to the identification with and mimicry of antisocial or pathological behaviors seen in online groups.
- *Intersubjectivity:* The shared fluid space of mutual understanding that is created between two minds in a genuine dialogue. This rich intersubjective field is robustly built in person but is thin, fragile, and prone to error in most forms of digital communication.

Chapter 10 References

Azar, B. (2005, October). How mimicry begat culture. *Monitor on Psychology, 36*(9), 42.
   Iacoboni,

M. (2009). Mirroring people: The new science of how we connect with others. Picador.

Ramachandran, V. S. (2011). *The tell-tale brain: A neuroscientist's quest for what makes us
   human.* W. W. Norton & Company.

Rizzolatti, G., & Craighero, L. (2004). The mirror-neuron system. *Annual Review of
   Neuroscience, 27*, 169–192.

11

Phantoms in the Machine

Projection and Paranoia in the Digital World

Consider this common adolescent scenario: a teenage girl sees an Instagram story showing her boyfriend at a party she was not invited to. He has not texted her back in an hour. Her internal monologue ignites: *He doesn't like me anymore. If he did, he would have texted. He's probably with Megan. She's been flirting with him. They probably hooked up. She's skinny and I'm fat. I'm such a loser.* Within minutes, a fantasy constructed from a few pixels and her own deepest insecurities feels like undeniable truth. She may lash out at him via text, post a cryptic and angry story of her own, or collapse into a state of depressive certainty that she has been rejected. This entire painful drama can emerge from a hyperactive imagination operating in a data vacuum. This is the world of projection, and social media is its perfect breeding ground.

The Data Void of Online Communication

As discussed in the previous chapter, face-to-face communication is extraordinarily data-rich. Our brains process hundreds of signals simultaneously: tone of voice, facial micro-expressions, posture, eye contact, even the rhythm of breathing. These cues help us test reality and form a reasonably accurate interpretation of another person's intentions and emotional state.

93

Online communication, particularly text-based interaction, is a data void. It is stripped of almost all these essential cues. A period at the end of a text can be read as sincerity, anger, or simple punctuation. The absence of an emoji can feel like a cold shoulder. A delay in response can feel like a deliberate slight. Into this void of missing information we do not inject reason; we inject fantasy.

Filling the Void with Projection

From a psychoanalytic perspective, projection is an unconscious defense mechanism in which we attribute our own unacceptable or unwanted feelings to another person. It is a way of disavowing parts of ourselves. For example, if I feel insecure I may, instead of tolerating that painful feeling, perceive others as critical or judgmental of me.

The data void of social media creates a perfect blank screen for these projections. The girl in our example projects her own insecurity about her worth and her fear of abandonment onto her boyfriend, creating a narrative of betrayal where none may exist. Her friends who do not "like" her post are not simply busy or offline; in her mind they are actively shunning her. This is more than a misunderstanding. It is an unconscious process of populating the ambiguous digital space with the phantoms of one's own inner world.

When Fantasy Feels Real: Projective Identification

This process can become even more complex and damaging through projective identification, a concept developed by Melanie Klein. It unfolds in three steps:

1. First an individual projects a feeling or part of themselves onto another person.

2. Next, they act toward that person in a way that provokes or pressures them into experiencing the projected feeling.
3. Finally, the original projector reabsorbs the feeling, but now it feels confirmed, as if it came from the other person.

For example, imagine a teen who feels insecure. In the first step, they project this insecurity outward and send their friend a passive-aggressive text: *"Guess you're too busy for me."* In the second step, the friend, who was simply in the shower, receives this text and feels irritated and unjustly accused. They reply, *"What are you talking about? I was busy."* In the third step, the original teen interprets this annoyed reply as proof of rejection, thinking, *Aha, I knew they were mad at me!*

What began as an internal insecurity has now been transformed into a seemingly real conflict. Neither teen is responding to the actual situation; instead, they both are caught in a cycle of projections. This is why text-based arguments can escalate so quickly online: each person is reacting not to reality but to distorted fantasies placed into the digital void.

What Can Be Done?

Helping teens navigate this digital maze of projection and paranoia requires teaching them the skills of reality testing, curious communication, and emotional self-awareness.

- **Teach the "Curiosity First" Rule.** When a digital interaction feels ambiguous or hurtful, the first impulse is to react with accusation. Coach your teen to replace accusation with curiosity. Instead of "Why are you ignoring me?," urge them to try, "Hey, just checking in. Is everything okay?" This simple shift can defuse countless conflicts by seeking data instead of confirming a fantasy.
- **Take it Offline.** Model and encourage the practice of moving any conversation that feels tense or confusing to a higher-bandwidth

medium. A simple rule: If a text conversation goes back and forth more than three times with negative emotion, it's time for a phone call. The auditory data of a voice can often clarify misunderstandings instantly.

- **Name the Phantom.** Help your teen build self-awareness by giving their projections a name. When they are spiraling about a perceived slight, say to them, "I hear your story about what's happening. Is it possible that the 'insecurity phantom' is telling you that story? What are the actual facts that we know for sure?" This helps them separate their internal anxiety from external reality.

- **Practice the "Pause."** The immediacy of digital communication encourages impulsive reactions. Teach your teen the power of the pause. When they receive a message that makes them feel angry or anxious, encourage them to put the phone down, walk away for ten minutes, and check in with their feelings before typing a response. This creates space for the rational brain to catch up with the emotional brain.

Key Neuroscience Concepts

- *The "Data Void":* A term describing the profound lack of nonverbal social data (tone of voice, facial expression, body language) in text-based communication. The brain is forced to fill in these missing pieces, often with its own biases and anxieties.
- *Reality Testing:* A key executive function, largely seated in the pre-frontal cortex, that is responsible for distinguishing between one's internal thoughts or fantasies and external, shared reality. This function is put under severe strain by ambiguous digital interactions.

Key Psychoanalytic Concepts

- *Projection:* An unconscious defense mechanism by which an individual attributes their own unacceptable or unwanted feelings (such as insecurity, anger, or fear) onto another person to avoid confronting those feelings within themselves. The "data void" of texting provides a perfect blank screen for these projections.
- *Projective Identification (Klein):* A more complex and interactive defense by which a person not only projects a feeling onto someone else but also, through their behavior, unconsciously coerces the other person into actually feeling and behaving that way, thus "confirming" the original projection in a toxic, self-fulfilling loop.
- *Digital Paranoia:* A state of heightened suspicion and mistrust fostered by the ambiguity of online communication. Without clear social cues, it becomes easy to interpret neutral or unclear messages (like a delayed response or a missing emoji) in the most negative possible light.

Chapter 11 References

Cataldo, I., Lepri, B., Neoh, M. J., & Esposito, G. (2021). Social media usage and development of psychiatric disorders in childhood and adolescence: A review. *Frontiers in Psychiatry, 11*, 508595.

Klein, M. (1946). Notes on some schizoid mechanisms. *International Journal of Psycho-Analysis, 27*, 99–110.

Sherman, L. E., Michikyan, M., & Greenfield, P. M. (2013). The effects of text, audio, video, and in-person communication on bonding between friends. *Cyberpsychology: Journal of Psychosocial Research on Cyberspace, 7*(2).

When the Screen Turns Deadly

Cyberbullying, Self-Harm, and Online Dangers

The psychological challenges discussed in the previous chapters—the overwhelmed ego, empathy deficits, and projections into the digital void—are not abstract concepts. They create profound vulnerabilities in the adolescent psyche. When these vulnerabilities collide with the most toxic aspects of the online world, the consequences can move from distressing to deadly. This chapter confronts the gravest risks of social media: those moments when the screen becomes a vector of life-altering harm and, in the most tragic cases, of death.

The 24/7 Schoolyard: The Unique Cruelty of Cyberbullying

Bullying has long been a painful feature of human social dynamics. For generations, however, children could find sanctuary at home. The schoolyard, the bus, the locker room—these were the primary arenas of torment. Cyberbullying has destroyed that sanctuary. Harassment now follows the victim into their bedroom, onto their pillow, and into their mind through the device in their pocket. This modern form of cruelty is uniquely damaging for several reasons:

- **Its Pervasiveness:** There is no escape. The bullying occurs across multiple platforms and can be relentless, leaving the victim's nervous system no time to recover.
- **Its Permanence:** A cruel comment whispered in a hallway eventually fades. An embarrassing photo, a humiliating video, or a vicious rumor posted online can be screenshotted, shared, and archived indefinitely, creating the potential for repeated retraumatization.
- **Its Vast Audience:** Humiliation is no longer confined to a small group of peers. It can be broadcast to the entire school or even go viral, magnifying shame to an unbearable degree.
- **Its Anonymity:** Bullies can hide behind faceless accounts, emboldening cruelty that might never surface in person. For the victim, this creates a chilling paranoia—the attack could be coming from anyone, anywhere.

Research confirms that victims of cyberbullying report higher levels of depression, anxiety, and suicidal ideation than victims of traditional bullying alone, precisely because of these unique and damaging features (Kowalski et al., 2014).

Echo Chambers of Pathology: Self-Harm and Pro–Eating Disorder Communities

For a teen who feels isolated, misunderstood, and ashamed, finding an online community that "understands" can feel like a lifeline. Tragically, for some this lifeline leads to an even more dangerous place. The internet is home to dark echo chambers that validate and even glorify self-destructive behaviors such as pro-anorexia ("pro-ana"), pro-bulimia ("pro-mia"), and self-harm forums.

From a psychoanalytic perspective, these communities provide a perverse form of mirroring and belonging. The teen who despises their body finds peers who celebrate emaciation. The adolescent coping with unbearable psychic pain through cutting finds a forum where scars are badges of strength rather than signs of distress. This distorted validation can be intoxicating, creating a feedback loop that pulls the teen deeper into pathology. Recovery then feels like betrayal, because the community has become a social mirror reflecting back a grotesque distortion of self.

From Sexting to Sextortion: The Landscape of Online Exploitation

Adolescence is a time of exploring sexuality and forming bonds, and in the digital age this exploration often involves texting and image sharing. While this can be a normal developmental step, it also opens the door to profound risks. An intimate photo shared in trust can be weaponized in an instant. It may reappear as "revenge porn" in the hands of a bitter ex-partner or become leverage in the hands of a predator.

Sextortion, a rapidly growing crime, often involves predators posing as peers. They convince a teen to share an explicit image, then threaten to distribute it unless their demands—typically for money or further images—are met (FBI, 2023). The psychological trauma is devastating. It combines extortion with profound shame and catastrophic betrayal, often leaving the victim paralyzed with fear, guilt, and despair.

The Contagion Effect: Suicidal Ideation in the Digital Age

The most tragic endpoint of these dangers is the loss of a young life to suicide. As discussed earlier, the links between heavy social media use and suicidality are alarming. One powerful mechanism is "suicide contagion," also known as the Werther effect, where exposure to suicide or suicidal behavior increases the risk of imitation.

Social media accelerates this contagion. Algorithms can trap vulnerable teens in a deadly feedback loop, serving them content that deepens hopelessness. Online sharing of methods, suicide notes, or glamorized portrayals of suicide spreads rapidly through peer networks, making the unthinkable imaginable. For the most vulnerable, platforms designed for connection can instead become conduits for despair.

What Can Be Done?

Responding to these serious problems requires vigilance, open communication, and a clear-eyed readiness to act decisively to protect your child's safety.

For Cyberbullying: Document, Block, and Report.

- *Document Everything:* Take screenshots of any harassing messages, posts, or profiles. This creates a record of evidence.
- *Don't Engage, Just Block:* Coach your teen that responding to a bully only fuels the fire. Do not engage. Use the block and mute functions liberally.
- *Report to the Platform and the School:* Report the offending content and accounts to the social media platform. If the bullying involves classmates, immediately report it to the school administration. Do not try to handle it alone.

For Dangerous Content: Monitor with Empathy.

- This is not about invasive spying, but about staying aware of the digital world your child inhabits. Have open conversations. Ask, "Are there any sites or trends online that make you feel uncomfortable or sad?" Create an atmosphere where they can talk to you about scary things without fear of immediate punishment.

For Exploitation: Create a "No-Shame Safety Plan."

- Have an explicit conversation with your teen. Tell them, "If you ever find yourself in a scary online situation where someone is threatening you or making you uncomfortable, I need you to promise me you will come to me for help. My first priority will be your safety. You will not be in trouble." Establishing this "no-shame" amnesty plan can be life-saving, as fear of punishment often prevents teens from disclosing exploitation.

For Suicide Risk: Ask the Question and Know the Resources.

- *Ask Directly:* It is a dangerous myth that asking about suicide plants the idea. If you are worried about your child, ask them directly and calmly, "Are you having thoughts about killing yourself?" This opens the door for a crucial conversation.
- *Know the Resources:* Have emergency resources ready. The 988 Suicide & Crisis Lifeline is available 24/7. Know the location of your nearest emergency room. If you believe your child is in immediate danger, do not wait. Seek help immediately.

Key Neuroscience Concepts

- *The "Data Void":* A term describing the profound lack of nonverbal social data (tone of voice, facial expression, body language) in text-based communication. The brain is forced to fill in these missing pieces, often with its own biases and anxieties.
- *Reality Testing:* A key executive function, largely seated in the pre-frontal cortex, that is responsible for distinguishing between one's internal thoughts or fantasies and external, consensual reality. This function is put under severe strain by ambiguous digital interactions.

Key Psychoanalytic Concepts

- *Projection:* An unconscious defense mechanism whereby an individual attributes their own unacceptable or unwanted feelings (such as insecurity, anger, or fear) onto another person to avoid confronting those feelings within themselves. The "data void" of texting provides a perfect blank screen for these projections.
- *Projective Identification (Klein):* A more complex and interactive defense by which a person not only projects a feeling onto someone else but, through their behavior, unconsciously coerces the other person into actually feeling and behaving that way, thus "confirming" the original projection in a toxic self-fulfilling loop.
- *Digital Paranoia:* A state of heightened suspicion and mistrust fostered by the ambiguity of online communication. Without clear social cues, it becomes easy to interpret neutral or unclear messages—a delayed response, a missing emoji—in the most negative light possible.

Chapter 12 References

Federal Bureau of Investigation (FBI). (2023). *Sextortion: What Parents and Caregivers Need to Know*. FBI.gov.

Hinduja, S., & Patchin, J. W. (2019). Connecting adolescent suicide to the severity of bullying and cyberbullying. *Journal of Criminology, Criminal Justice, Law & Society, 20*(1), 68–80.

Kowalski, R. M., Giumetti, G. W., Schroeder, A. N., & Lattanner, M. R. (2014). Bullying in the digital age: A critical review and meta-analysis of cyberbullying research among youth. *Psychological Bulletin, 140*(4), 1073–1137.

Twenge, J. M., Cooper, A. B., Joiner, T. E., Duffy, M. E., & Binau, S. G. (2019). Age, period, and cohort trends in mood disorder indicators and suicide-related outcomes in a nationally representative dataset, 2005–2017. *Journal of Abnormal Psychology, 128*(3), 185–199.

The Shared Psychosis

When Social Media Becomes Reality

In clinical practice, we occasionally see a rare phenomenon called *folie à deux*, or "shared psychosis," in which one person's delusion is transmitted to another. The dominant partner, suffering from a primary psychotic disorder, imposes their delusion onto a more passive, suggestible one, who then comes to believe it as truth. In the age of social media we are witnessing a terrifying expansion of this phenomenon: a *folie à plusieurs*—a madness of many—where entire groups are swept up into a shared delusion and walled off from consensual reality.

The Algorithm as a Surrogate Parent

For many, social media has become a kind of surrogate parent. It is where we learn what to want, who to fear, what counts as beautiful, and what to treat as truth. For the adolescent brain—still in the midst of synaptic pruning—this is especially consequential. Neural pathways reinforced by the algorithm are strengthened, while those left unused fade away.

When a teen's primary source of information is a TikTok feed or a YouTube rabbit hole, the algorithm effectively becomes the architect of their worldview. The "parent" in this case is not a loving figure but an impersonal system designed to maximize attention. What it nurtures is not curiosity or resilience, but whatever content drives the most engagement.

Projection at a Societal Scale

Projection, as we have seen in interpersonal dynamics, occurs when we disown painful feelings and situate them in someone else. Social media magnifies this process at the level of entire groups. The algorithms divide users into echo chambers and filter bubbles, creating ideological tribes that rarely encounter opposing views.

Inside these digital tribes, projection runs rampant. The "other side" is not simply mistaken—it becomes evil, stupid, or even dangerous. This group-level projection dehumanizes opponents, eroding the possibility of dialogue and making conflict feel inevitable. Within such an environment, conspiracy theories thrive. The belief that vaccines are tools of social control or that elections are routinely "stolen" does not arise in isolation. It is born of repeated projection, validated endlessly by others in the same echo chamber, until fantasy hardens into what feels like fact.

Groupthink and the Collapse of Reality Testing

Once a group has adopted a shared delusion, powerful psychological forces lock it in place. Questioning the narrative becomes betrayal. Dissenters risk ostracism, a form of social death that can feel unbearable. The pressure to conform is immense.

At this stage, reality testing collapses. Only evidence that confirms the group's belief is allowed. Anything contradictory is dismissed as "fake news" or propaganda from the enemy. Within this sealed mental environment, even the most bizarre ideas can take root and spread. The group has constructed its own reality, and social media algorithms happily reinforce it, since keeping people engaged—angry, fearful, and glued to their feeds—is the most profitable outcome. The result is not just individual distortion but a collective one: social media as a primary vector of dangerous misinformation and the erosion of a shared, fact-based reality.

What Can Be Done?

Resisting the pull of shared digital delusions requires developing strong skills in media literacy and intellectual humility.

- **Perform a "Feed Audit."** Regularly review who you follow and what information sources are shaping your worldview. Make a conscious effort to follow credible journalists, scientists, and thinkers from a wide range of perspectives, including those with whom you disagree. This is an active inoculation against the intellectual poison of an echo chamber.
- **Practice the "Principle of Charity."** The principle of charity suggests that when interpreting someone else's statement, you should assume the most rational and reasonable interpretation possible. Before assuming someone from the "other side" is evil or stupid, try to construct the strongest possible version of their argument. This fosters intellectual humility and resists the dehumanizing tendency of projection.
- **Verify Before You Amplify.** Make it a personal rule to never share, "like," or forward a piece of shocking information without first attempting to verify it from a credible, primary source. Teach this skill to your teens. This single habit, if adopted widely, could significantly slow the spread of misinformation.
- **Prioritize In-Person Dialogue.** Whenever possible, discuss difficult or polarizing topics with people face-to-face, especially with those who have differing views. The rich data of in-person communication—the nonverbal cues, the shared humanity—acts as a powerful corrective to the distortions and projections that run rampant online.

Key Neuroscience Concepts

- *Filter Bubbles:* The state where an algorithm selectively guesses what information a user would like to see based on their past behavior, effectively isolating them from differing viewpoints and creating a personalized, self-validating reality.
- *Neural Correlates of Group Identity:* The neurological phenomenon whereby our brains experience a reward response when our "in-group" is affirmed and a threat response when it is challenged. Algorithms exploit this by feeding us content that reinforces our tribal identity.

Key Psychoanalytic Concepts

- *Folie à Plusieurs ("Madness of Many"):* An expansion of the clinical concept of a shared psychosis (*folie à deux*). In the digital age, this refers to how entire online groups can become captured by a shared delusion, reinforcing it until it feels like an objective truth.
- *Societal Projection:* The process by which a group projects its own fears, aggressions, or other unwanted traits onto a rival "out-group." This dehumanizes the other side and is a key psychological driver of political polarization and conspiracy theories.
- *Groupthink:* The psychological drive for consensus within a group that can cause individuals to set aside their own personal beliefs or ignore contradictory evidence in order to maintain group cohesion.

Chapter 13 References

Cataldo, I., Lepri, B., Neoh, M. J., & Esposito, G. (2021). Social media usage and de-velopment of psychiatric disorders in childhood and adolescence: A review. *Frontiers in Psychiatry, 11*, 508–595.

Janis, I. L. (1972). *Victims of groupthink: A psychological study of foreign-policy decisions and fiascoes.* Houghton Mifflin.

Sunstein, C. R. (2017). *#Republic: Divided democracy in the age of social media.* Princeton University Press.

PART 3

Adulthood and Aging

14

The Adult in the Machine

Addiction, Burnout, and the Search for Connection

The addictive allure of games, videos, and social media does not vanish at the stroke of one's eighteenth birthday. For many adults, the digital habits formed in adolescence persist and intertwine with the complex responsibilities of work, family, and relationships. In our clinical practices we regularly see adults whose lives are quietly, and sometimes catastrophically, derailed by their relationship with screens.

The Escape into Digital Worlds

The structure of adult life, with its greater freedom and lack of supervision, can create the perfect conditions for a latent screen dependency to blossom into a full-blown gaming addiction. This is now formally recognized by both the American Psychiatric Association and the World Health Organization as Internet Gaming Disorder.

One clinical case involved a man in his early thirties who had effectively lost the entire decade of his twenties to a video game. To cover up his habit, he fabricated a story about working a night job, hiding his nightly, multihour gaming sessions from friends and family.

This escape is not confined to solitary gaming. In couples therapy we often encounter partners who feel they are in competition with a device. One spouse may describe the other prioritizing a video game, an endless news feed, or a social media scroll over quality time together. This digital "affair" can be devastating. The neglected partner feels ignored and devalued, and resentment and loneliness gradually erode communication and intimacy.

The same dynamic plays out with online pornography, now accessible around the clock.

The progression often follows a familiar path: what begins as a private indulgence can evolve into a compulsion that disrupts work, damages relationships, and creates a cycle of shame, anxiety, and depression. In some cases the solution has been surprisingly simple. Several patients found that their problem stemmed largely from isolation during remote work. Returning to the structure of an office environment, where such behaviors were less possible, was enough to break the cycle. This illustrates a crucial truth: sometimes the issue is not deep-seated pathology, but the way we regulate our time and shape our environments.

The Erosion of Rest and Focus

Even for adults without a clear addiction, screens exert a steady toll on well-being. Taking a phone or tablet to bed has become almost universal. We tell ourselves we are "winding down," but in reality we are doing the opposite. The brain is not reflecting at this time; it is processing.

Whether it is a work email or a drama series, the content stimulates the mind, creating cognitive and emotional arousal that undermines sleep (Hale & Guan, 2015). Streaming platforms have exacerbated this with autoplay features, eliminating the small pause of pressing a button that might allow the prefrontal cortex to intervene and say, *It's 2 a.m., it's time to stop.*

A newer assault on focus comes from the very devices designed to optimize health. Smartwatches and fitness trackers, while marketed as wellness tools, can create a state of constant cognitive disruption.

Pings, vibrations, and data streams demand attention, fragmenting concentration and creating a mental burden that can outweigh any physical benefits.

The Complication of Intimacy

The landscape of modern dating has been reshaped by apps that often prioritize instant gratification over the slow, uncertain process of building connection. This reversal of the traditional human approach to romance leaves many young adults, especially those already socially anxious, feeling bewildered and inadequate. They struggle to navigate a world where first encounters are transactional and relationships feel disposable.

The fear of intimacy has given rise to a new language of "situation-ships" where adults avoid naming the exact nature of the arrangement. Commitment itself becomes so fraught that conversations are reduced to questions of exclusivity: Are we official or not, are our profiles still active or deleted? What should be a space of tenderness and discovery instead becomes saturated with projection, paranoia, anxiety, and insecurity. Love, one of life's most precious opportunities, is too often sabotaged at its earliest stages, leaving behind rejection and the quiet destruction of ruminating over what might have been.

In extreme cases, this has led to seeking out sex workers not for pleasure, but as a form of off-label therapy: a way to experience intimacy without the risk of rejection or the demands of genuine emotional vulnerability. Sex has lost much of its meaning as the deepest expression of love between two people. Instead, it has been recast as the prize after the hunt, a confirmation of one's desirability. For many, this need for validation repeats endlessly, turning sex into little more than a ritual of pursuit and reward. Over time, the hunt and the act itself become so tightly intertwined that intimacy in the context of a loving, stable relationship feels difficult, even impossible. The cycle of novelty, conquest, and reward replaces genuine connection. What appears on the surface as indulgence is, more often than not, a desperate attempt to bridge the widening gap between digital connection and authentic human closeness.

What Can Be Done?

For adults, managing screen use is an act of conscious self-regulation and boundary-setting. It requires acknowledging the powerful design of these technologies and actively choosing to prioritize one's own well-being.

- **Create a "Digital Commute."** For those who work from home, the lack of a physical transition between work and personal life can lead to endless screen time. Create a ritual to bookend your day. This could be a 15-minute walk before you start work and another when you finish. This practice creates a mental boundary, signaling to your brain that the workday is over and it's time to disengage.
- **Schedule "Analog" Time with Your Partner.** If you find yourself in a relationship where screens are causing distance, be proactive. Schedule specific, recurring, tech-free time together. This could be a nightly walk after dinner, a weekly board-game night, or a Sunday morning coffee date. The key is to make this connection time as nonnegotiable as you would a work meeting.
- **Use Dating Apps with Intention.** If you use dating apps, do so with clear boundaries. Set a timer for 20 to 30 minutes of use, and then log off. Focus on moving promising connections from the app to a real-world interaction (like a phone call or a coffee meeting) relatively quickly to avoid getting trapped in an endless cycle of superficial texting, compulsive app checking and frequent one-night stands.

- **Reclaim Your Bedroom.** Your bedroom should be for sleep and intimacy only. Buy a physical alarm clock and charge all your devices in another room overnight. This single change can dramatically improve sleep quality and create more opportunities for connection with a partner.

Key Neuroscience Concepts

- *Internet Gaming Disorder:* A formally recognized behavioral addiction in which the brain's reward pathways are hijacked by the dopamine feedback loops of video games, leading to compulsive use that can derail an adult's career, relationships, and health.
- *Cognitive Arousal and Sleep:* Engaging with emotionally or intellectually stimulating screen content before bed keeps the brain in a state of high alert, suppressing melatonin and preventing the transition into the deep, restorative stages of sleep necessary for mental and physical health.
- *Continuous Partial Attention:* A state induced by constant notifications from devices like smartwatches in which the brain is never fully focused on a single task. This degrades the ability to perform deep work and increases cognitive fatigue.

Key Psychoanalytic Concepts

- *The Screen as Psychic Retreat:* The use of digital worlds (gaming, porn, social media) as an unconscious escape from the anxieties and responsibilities of adult life, such as professional pressure, financial stress, or the demands of relational intimacy.
- *Technoference in Partnerships:* The dynamic in which one partner's absorption in a device acts as a "digital affair," creating a painful relational triangle that starves the partnership of presence and fosters deep feelings of resentment and loneliness.
- *Failure of Adult Self-Regulation:* How the unstructured nature of modern life (e.g., working from home) can expose and amplify underlying difficulties with self-discipline, allowing screen-based compulsions to flourish in the absence of external social constraints.

Chapter 14 References

Hale, L., & Guan, S. (2015). Screen time and sleep among school-aged children and adolescents: A systematic literature review. *Sleep Medicine Reviews, 21*, 50–58.

Kardefelt-Winther, D., et al. (2017). The association between problematic video gaming and gaming motivations, sleep disturbance, and academic performance among adolescents and young adults. *Journal of Behavioral Addictions, 6*(4), 479–488.

World Health Organization. (2018). *International classification of diseases for mortality and morbidity statistics (11th Revision).*

15

The Plastic Brain

Is the Damage Reversible?

Throughout this book we have painted a concerning picture of how the digital world can negatively impact brain development and psychological well-being. A natural and pressing question arises: Is this damage permanent? Is a generation raised on screens destined for a lifetime of distraction and disconnection? The answer, rooted in one of the most hopeful discoveries in modern neuroscience, is a qualified but resounding "no." The reason for this optimism is the principle of neuroplasticity.

The Brain That Changes Itself

For most of the twentieth century, the prevailing view was that the adult brain is essentially fixed, like a piece of hardware with unchangeable wiring. We now know this is profoundly mistaken. Neuroplasticity is the brain's remarkable lifelong ability to reorganize itself by forming new neural connections in response to experience, learning, and injury (Mateos-Aparicio & Rodríguez-Moreno, 2019).

The evidence for this is dramatic. Studies of musicians show that they have larger cortical representations for the fingers of their playing hand, the result of thousands of hours of practice (Elbert et al., 1995). Seminal work by neuroscientist V.S. Ramachandran (1993) demonstrated that after an amputation, the neurons that once received input from the missing limb can rapidly rewire themselves to respond to stimulation from other parts of the body. This is not a metaphor. The brain physically changes its structure and function based on the demands placed upon it.

This principle is also the foundation of modern psychotherapy. When someone engages in therapy to overcome trauma, they are not just "talking about their problems." They are participating in a process that can rewire neural circuits in the limbic system and prefrontal cortex, creating healthier pathways for emotional regulation and memory (Cozzalino, 2017).

A Double-Edged Sword

This same capacity for change is what makes the digital environment so powerful, for better and for worse. The adolescent brain that is constantly bombarded with the rapid-fire stimulation of TikTok is wiring itself for distraction. Neural pathways for sustained focus and deep thinking are pruned from lack of use. Conversely, an adolescent who devotes time to learning a complex skill such as coding, music, or chess is strengthening pathways for logic, memory, and concentration.

The brain adapts to whatever it practices most. That fact gives us immense hope. It means that the person addicted to social media can, through new behaviors and consistent effort, forge new neural pathways and gradually break free from the addictive cycle. A brain shaped by distraction can, with time and commitment, be reshaped by focus.

However, this hope must be tempered with realism. Plasticity exists throughout life, but it is not limitless. There are "sensitive periods" in development, particularly in childhood and adolescence, when the brain is most malleable and certain skills are most easily acquired. For instance, while it is possible to learn a new language as an adult, it is far more difficult than for a young child. Similarly, while an adult can work to overcome the effects of early relational trauma, the process requires far more effort than building a secure attachment from the beginning.

The damage is not necessarily irreversible. But the work of repair grows harder with each passing year. This is the paradox of neuroplasticity: it is our greatest source of hope, but also a reminder of the urgency to intervene early, intentionally, and consistently.

What Can Be Done?

We can all become active gardeners of our own neural pathways. The principles for promoting positive neuroplasticity are clear and accessible to everyone.

- **Embrace Novelty.** The brain is stimulated by newness. Learning any new skill, no matter how small, creates new neural connections. This could be trying a new recipe, taking a different route on your daily walk, or tackling a new type of puzzle. Actively seek out experiences that push you out of your routine.
- **Prioritize Focused Attention.** Neuroplasticity requires focused attention. When you practice a new skill, whether it's a musical instrument or meditation, it's the quality of your focus that drives the rewiring. "Single-tasking" is a powerful tool for brain change.
- **Get Moving.** Physical exercise is one of the most potent promoters of neuroplasticity. Cardiovascular exercise increases blood flow to the brain and stimulates the release of brain-derived neurotrophic factor (BDNF), a protein that acts like fertilizer for new neurons.
- **Sleep.** It is during deep sleep that the brain consolidates learning and clears out metabolic waste. Consistent high-quality sleep is not a luxury; it is the essential maintenance work that allows for positive brain change to occur.

Key Neuroscience Concepts

- *Neuroplasticity:* The brain's fundamental lifelong ability to change its own structure and function in response to experience, learning, and behavior. This is the biological basis for hope that the negative effects of screen time are not necessarily permanent.
- *Hebbian Theory ("Neurons that fire together, wire together"):* The principle that every time we repeat a thought or action, we strengthen the neural pathway associated with it. This explains how both good habits (like mindfulness) and bad habits (like compulsive phone checking) become ingrained.
- *Critical/Sensitive Periods:* Windows of time in development (especially childhood and adolescence) when the brain is most plastic and best able to learn certain skills. While change is possible in adulthood, it often requires more conscious effort to rewire established neural pathways.

Key Psychoanalytic Concepts

- *Psychotherapy as Brain Change:* The modern understanding that engaging in talk therapy is not just a psychological process, but a biological one. A strong therapeutic relationship can help a person build new, healthier neural pathways for emotional regulation and self-awareness.
- *The Capacity for Reintegration:* The ego's ability, through insight and effort, to heal from past wounds and develop new, more adaptive ways of coping with reality.
- *The Reality Principle (in Adulthood):* Freud's concept that the mature ego learns to delay gratification and manage its impulses according to the demands of reality. Choosing to put down the phone to focus on a long-term goal is a classic example of the reality principle in action.

Chapter 15 References

Cozzolino, L. J. (2017). *The neuroscience of psychotherapy: Healing the social brain* (3rd ed.). W. W. Norton & Company.

Elbert, T., Pantev, C., Wienbruch, C., Rockstroh, B., & Taub, E. (1995). Increased cortical representation of the fingers of the left hand in string players. *Science, 270*(5234), 305–307.

Mateos-Aparicio, P., & Rodríguez-Moreno, A. (2019). The impact of studying brain plasticity. *Frontiers in Cellular Neuroscience, 13*, 66.

Ramachandran, V. S. (1993). Behavioral and magnetoencephalographic correlates of plasticity in the adult human brain. *Proceedings of the National Academy of Sciences of the United States of America, 90*(22), 10413–10420.

16

Reclaiming Our Minds

Strategies for Change at Every Level

If you saw a toddler about to wander into a busy street, you would not hesitate. You would not pause to weigh pros and cons. You would act immediately to pull them back from danger. The argument of this book is that our children are in a similar state of peril. They are wandering into a digital environment that is fundamentally hostile to their healthy development. The time for passive observation is over. We must act.

Changing a force as powerful as the modern tech industry can feel hopeless. But if humans can land rovers on Mars and edit the building blocks of life, we can surely redesign a smartphone app. This is not a technological problem; it is a problem of political and social will. The solution requires a multilevel approach: demanding systemic change, strengthening communities, and making conscious choices in our own homes.

The Societal Level: A New Code for Tech

The current model of self-regulation in the tech industry has been a catastrophic failure. Platforms have proven they will not prioritize the well-being of their users over profits. Therefore we must demand a new social contract, enforced through robust government regulation. Nearly every other industry with direct impact on health and safety—from food and medicine to cars and airplanes—is subject to safety standards and oversight. Tech should be no exception. This could include:

- **Banning Manipulative Design.** Features designed solely to foster addiction, such as endless scroll and autoplay for children's content, should be prohibited.
- **Requiring Algorithmic Transparency.** Companies should be required to disclose how their algorithms operate and what data they use to target users. Independent researchers must have access to this data to study the platforms' societal impact.
- **Creating a Digital FDA.** An independent government agency should be empowered to review new digital products for safety before they are released, particularly to children.
- **Holding Platforms Liable.** Section 230 of the Communications Decency Act, which grants platforms broad immunity for user content, must be reformed. Platforms that knowingly amplify harmful content through their algorithms should be held legally responsible for the consequences.

The Community Level: Education and Alternatives

Our schools and local communities are essential to building a healthier digital culture.

- **Core Curriculum Media Literacy.** Media literacy and digital citizenship should not be occasional workshops. They should be core subjects taught from elementary school through high school. Students must understand how algorithms work, how to identify misinformation, and how to protect their own mental health online.
- **Promoting Offline Alternatives.** If we want kids to put down their phones, we need to give them something better to pick up.

This means robust investment in school sports, arts programs, libraries, and community centers. Offline spaces must be made compelling again.

The Family Level: The Last Line of Defense

Ultimately, the most important line of defense is the family. As Tristan Harris, co-founder of the Center for Humane Technology, has warned, if we cannot agree on a shared reality "we are toast." Families are where children first learn about reality, values, and connection. Parents must be willing to set and enforce firm, consistent boundaries around technology use. This is not about authoritarian control; it is about loving leadership. It means creating a family tech plan, modeling healthy habits, and choosing presence over distraction. It is not easy, but it is among the most important responsibilities of modern parenting.

What Can Be Done?

This chapter is a call to action. Change requires a concerted effort at every level of society. Here is a summary of where to begin.

- **At the Societal Level: Become an Advocate.** Support and vote for political candidates who take the issue of tech regulation seriously. Support organizations like the Center for Humane Technology that are fighting for a healthier digital world. Demand that our leaders treat digital safety with the same seriousness as physical safety.
- **At the Community Level: Get Involved.** Advocate for robust media literacy programs in your local schools. Support your local library and community centers. Coach a sports team or volunteer with a youth group. Help build the compelling offline world that our children so desperately need.

- **At the Family Level: Lead by Example.** Create a family tech plan and stick to it. Enforce tech-free dinners and bedrooms. Model the behavior you want to see in your children. Prioritize family time that is free from the intrusion of screens.
- **At the Individual Level: Be Mindful.** Take stock of your own digital habits. Turn off nonessential notifications. Use apps to track your screen time. Practice screen free time. Be the conscious, intentional user of your technology, not the other way around.

Key Neuroscience Concepts

- *The "Attention Economy":* The modern business model, particularly in tech, that treats human attention as a scarce commodity to be captured and monetized. This model is inherently in conflict with individual well-being.
- *Persuasive Design:* The practice of designing technology to deliberately influence human behavior by exploiting cognitive biases, such as our need for social validation or our fear of missing out.

Key Psychoanalytic Concepts

- *Agency and Will:* The ego's capacity to make conscious, deliberate choices in the face of unconscious pulls and external pressures. The act of mindfully managing one's technology use is an expression of psychological agency.
- *The Societal Superego:* An extension of the concept of the individual's moral conscience (the superego). This refers to our collective responsibility to demand and create rules, regulations, and ethical standards to protect society from harmful forces, including exploitative technology.
- *The Primacy of Reality:* A core tenet of mental health is the ability to distinguish internal fantasy from external reality. A primary goal for our society must be to fight for a shared, fact-based reality by resisting the fracturing forces of misinformation and digital echo chambers.

Chapter 16 References

Harris, T. (Co-founder, Center for Humane Technology). (2020). *The Social Dilemma* [Documentary Film]. Netflix.

Hinduja, S., & Patchin, J. W. (2021). *Addressing the challenges of social media: A primer for parents, educators, and communities.* Cyberbullying Research Center.

U.S. Surgeon General. (2023). *Social Media and Youth Mental Health: The U.S. Surgeon General's Advisory.* U.S. Department of Health and Human Service

17

The Aging Brain

Navigating Natural Changes in the Digital Era

We rarely think about the brain's development until it interrupts us. We misplace our keys, blank on a familiar name, or notice a parent struggling in ways they never have before. These moments can be jarring reminders that the brain, like the rest of the body, undergoes a profound and normal process of change as we age. Understanding these changes is the first step to navigating them with clarity and grace.

Changes to the Hardware: Structure and Speed

The adult brain is not static. After reaching its peak in young adulthood, it begins a slow and steady process of physical change. Neuroimaging studies show that the brain gradually shrinks in volume with age, a process known as brain atrophy. This shrinkage is not uniform.

Some regions are more vulnerable than others, particularly the prefrontal cortex, which governs executive function, and the hippocampus, which is critical for memory formation (Fjell & Walhovd, 2010).

At the same time, the brain's communication system becomes less efficient. The myelin sheath that insulates neurons can degrade, slowing the speed of electrical signals. This reduced connectivity makes multitasking more difficult and can affect motor coordination. For an older adult this might appear as difficulty following a fast-paced conversation while trying to read a menu—a task that may have felt effortless decades earlier.

Shifts in the Software: Hormones and Neurotransmitters

The chemical environment of the brain also changes with age. Key hormones that support neuroprotection decline. Estrogen, which helps maintain synaptic health, drops significantly during menopause, affecting memory. Testosterone, linked to spatial abilities, gradually decreases in older men. At the same time, cortisol, the body's primary stress hormone, often rises with age.

Chronically elevated cortisol can be toxic to the hippocampus, damaging memory and creating a vicious cycle in which the stress of cognitive lapses produces more cortisol, which in turn worsens those lapses.

Neurotransmitters also decline. Reduced dopamine can diminish mood, motivation, and the ability to take pleasure in life, sometimes leading to apathy. Lower serotonin can contribute to depression, anxiety, and sleep difficulties. These chemical shifts form part of the emotional landscape of aging, shaping how older adults experience both themselves and the world.

Compounding Risk Factors and Dementia

The health of the brain in later life is closely linked to overall physical health across the lifespan. Chronic conditions such as high blood pressure, diabetes, and heart disease can damage blood vessels, reduce blood flow to the brain, and increase the risk of both cognitive decline and vascular dementia.

It is important to note that while some degree of decline in cognitive function is a normal part of aging, dementia is not. Dementia is a disease state marked by a decline severe enough to interfere with daily life. The most common form, Alzheimer's disease, is associated with the accumulation of amyloid plaques and tau tangles in the brain. Today it affects more than six million Americans, a number projected to more than double by 2060 (Alzheimer's Association, 2023).

What Can Be Done?

While we cannot stop the aging process, we can take active steps to promote brain health and build cognitive reserve, which is the mind's way of compensating for neurological damage.

- **"Use It or Lose It."** The brain retains some plasticity throughout life. The best way to maintain it is to challenge it. Encourage life-long learning: taking a class at a community college, learning a new language with an app, mastering a new skill like painting or playing an instrument. Even engaging with complex puzzles like crosswords or Sudoku helps maintain neural pathways.
- **Prioritize Physical Health.** The link between physical and brain health is undeniable. Regular cardiovascular exercise increases blood flow to the brain. A healthy diet, such as the Mediterranean diet, has been shown to protect against cognitive decline. And crucially, managing chronic health conditions like high blood pressure and diabetes is a primary form of brain care.
- **Stay Socially Engaged.** Social connection is a powerful cognitive enhancer. Engaging in conversation, debating ideas, and sharing experiences with others is a complex workout for the brain. This is one area where technology, when used intentionally, can be a powerful tool for the elderly.
- **Manage Stress.** Given the damaging effects of chronically high cortisol levels, stress management is key. Practices like meditation, deep breathing, yoga, or spending time in nature can help regulate the body's stress response and protect the brain.

Key Neuroscience Concepts

- *Brain Atrophy:* The natural and expected age-related shrinkage of the brain's volume. This process is particularly pronounced in the prefrontal cortex (affecting executive function) and the hippocampus (affecting memory formation and retrieval).
- *Myelin Degradation:* The gradual breakdown of the fatty myelin sheath that insulates neurons. This degradation slows the brain's processing speed, reduces communication efficiency between brain regions, and makes complex tasks like multitasking more difficult.
- *Cortisol and Neurotoxicity:* The tendency for levels of the stress hormone cortisol to increase with age. Chronically high levels of cortisol can be toxic to the brain, specifically damaging cells in the hippocampus and further impairing memory.
- *Cognitive Reserve:* The concept that a lifetime of engaging in mentally stimulating activities (like learning, problem-solving, and social interaction) builds a buffer of redundant neural connections that can help protect the brain from the functional impact of age-related damage.

Key Psychoanalytic Concepts

- *Escaping Uncomfortable Feelings:* The digital world offers a powerful way to avoid difficult emotions, anxieties, or feelings of inadequacy that come with adult responsibilities. Instead of facing these feelings, the mind escapes into a more predictable and often instantly rewarding digital space.
- *Seeking False Control and Power:* In games or on social media, we can often feel a sense of mastery, power, or immediate validation that might be missing in our complex adult lives. This taps into an unconscious desire for omnipotence, a feeling of being all-powerful, which provides temporary relief from real-world frustrations.
- *Avoiding Real Relationships:* Sometimes the digital world becomes a "safer" alternative to real-life relationships, which can be messy and unpredictable. It allows for a form of connection that avoids the risks of rejection or deep emotional vulnerability.

Chapter 17 References

Alzheimer's Association. (2023). 2023 Alzheimer's disease facts and figures. *Alzheimer's & Dementia, 19*(4).

Fjell, A. M., & Walhovd, K. B. (2010). Structural brain changes in aging: courses, causes and cognitive consequences. *Reviews in the Neurosciences, 21*(3), 187–221.

Sapolsky, R. M. (2000). Glucocorticoids and cognitive impairment. *Archives of General Psychiatry, 57*(10), 925–927.

18

The Double-Edged Screen

Perils and Promises for the Elderly

For older adults, the digital screen is a double-edged sword. On one hand, it can magnify the challenges of aging and quietly chip away at health and well-being. On the other, it can be a lifeline, offering connection, stimulation, and independence in ways that were unimaginable even a generation ago. For seniors and the people who love them, learning how to balance these two realities is one of the defining tasks of modern aging.

The Perils of the Screen

The Sedentary Life

It's easy to imagine the appeal: an older adult with sore knees or limited mobility settles into a favorite chair, the television humming along for hours. The comfort is real, but so are the risks. Too much passive screen time is linked to poorer physical health, and research suggests that it may even contribute to cognitive decline (Raichlen et al., 2023). Whether or not TV itself is the culprit, the problem is clear: the more hours spent sitting still, the less opportunity the brain and body have to stay active and engaged.

The Threat of Scams

Anyone who has ever watched a parent or grandparent open an email from a "bank" they don't use knows the fear in this territory. Older adults are frequent targets for scams, not because they are careless, but because loneliness, trust, and slower processing speed can make them vulnerable. From romance scams that prey on the desire for companionship to fraudulent calls and emails seeking financial information, the digital world can sometimes feel less like a bridge and more like a trap.

Information Overload and Anxiety

Think of a retiree sitting with the TV on in the background all day, switching between 24-hour news channels. The stream of sensational headlines and frightening imagery can take a toll. Because the aging brain processes information more slowly, it can be harder to filter the noise. The most vivid and dramatic stories stick, creating the impression that danger lurks everywhere. The result is often increased anxiety, restlessness, and even reluctance to leave home.

The "Quick Fix" for Loneliness

Loneliness in later life is profound, and screens can sometimes provide quick comfort. But the "comfort" isn't always healthy. Online shopping can become compulsive, filling the quiet with packages at the door but also straining finances. In some cases, it can escalate into hoarding, making living spaces unsafe. What begins as a way to ease loneliness can spiral into a cycle that deepens it.

The Promises of the Screen

A Bridge Across Distance

At the same time, technology can bring immeasurable joy. Anyone who has ever watched an older adult's face light up at a video call with a grandchild knows this truth. For someone who can no longer travel easily, FaceTime and Zoom are more than apps. They are windows to birthdays, holiday dinners, and ordinary afternoons, keeping families knitted together across miles. For many, these small glowing rectangles are a reason to get up in the morning and stay connected to life.

A Gym for the Brain

Not all screen time is passive. When older adults use technology actively, it can be a true workout for the mind. Learning how to navigate a new app, organizing digital photos, or even troubleshooting a printer problem demands problem-solving and creativity. These everyday challenges strengthen neural pathways and help build cognitive reserve, much as exercise builds muscle. Used intentionally, screens can become tools for keeping the mind sharp.

Empowerment and Independence

One of the most remarkable gifts of the internet is the sense of independence it can restore. Seniors can look up health information, manage medications, or access support groups without waiting on a doctor's office to call back. Smart home technology adds another layer of freedom. Voice-activated assistants, automated lighting, and fall detection systems can help older adults live safely in their own homes for longer. For someone who has spent a lifetime caring for others, being able to maintain autonomy can be a profound source of dignity and self-worth.

For older adults, screens can be both thief and gift. They can steal time, health, and peace of mind, but they can also return connection, stimulation, and independence. The challenge is not to eliminate screens but to use them wisely, with balance and intention. For caregivers and loved ones, that means helping seniors find the sweet spot: enough technology to enrich life, but not so much that it replaces it.

What Can Be Done?

The goal is to help older adults harness the immense benefits of technology while protecting them from its potential harms.

- **Promote Digital Literacy.** Offer or find classes specifically designed for seniors that teach basic computer skills, online safety, and how to spot scams. Many local libraries and senior centers provide these resources. This builds confidence and reduces vulnerability.
- **Use Tech to Facilitate Real-World Connection.** Technology should be a bridge to the real world, not a substitute for it. Use social media or email to organize a real-life book club, a weekly walking group, or a get-together with old friends.
- **Simplify and Secure the Tech.** Set up devices with large fonts, simple interfaces, and strong security software. Preprogram important contacts into a smartphone or tablet. The easier the technology is to use, the more likely it is to be a source of connection rather than frustration.
- **Focus on the "Why."** When introducing new technology, focus on the benefit it provides, not the technology itself. The goal isn't to "learn the iPad"; the goal is to "see your grandchildren's faces every day." This provides the intrinsic motivation needed to overcome the initial learning curve.

Key Neuroscience Concepts

- *The Availability Heuristic (in the Elderly):* The mental shortcut where we judge risk based on the most easily recalled information. This can make older adults particularly vulnerable to the 24/7 news cycle, which often highlights sensational and frightening events, leading to a heightened and often distorted sense of personal danger.
- *Cognitive Stimulation vs. Passive Consumption:* The crucial neurological distinction between actively engaging the brain (e.g., by learning a new app or video chatting with family) and passively consuming content (e.g., watching daytime TV). The former builds cognitive reserve, while the latter may correlate with cognitive decline.

Key Psychoanalytic Concepts

- *The Screen as Lifeline:* For an isolated older person, technology can serve as a vital connection to the outside world, staving off the profound psychic pain of loneliness and providing access to family, friends, and community.
- *Autonomy vs. Dependence:* How technology, particularly smart-home and AI-powered tools, can support an older person's sense of independence and self-sufficiency. This feeling of agency is a powerful psychological buffer against the depression that can accompany the loss of a physical function.
- *Digital Vulnerability:* How the psychological needs of later life—such as the desire for connection, companionship, or a sense of purpose—can be exploited by online scammers, leading to significant financial and emotional trauma.

Chapter 18 References

Anderson, M., & Perrin, A. (2017). *Tech adoption climbs among older adults.* Pew Research Center.

Raichlen, D. A., Sayre, M. K., et al. (2023). Sedentary behavior and incident dementia among older adults. *JAMA, 330*(10), 934–941.

Tversky, A., & Kahneman, D. (1973). Availability: A heuristic for judging frequency and probability. *Cognitive Psychology, 5*(2), 207–232.

19

The Search for Integrity vs. Despair

Aging, Screens, and the Weight of Reflection

Aging is often framed in our society as a story of decline and loss. Psychoanalyst Erik Erikson offered a more profound and hopeful perspective. He argued that the elderly phase of life is not an ending but the final, crucial stage of development. It is a time for reflection, integration, and the culmination of a life's meaning. The central psychosocial crisis of this stage is *Integrity vs. Despair.*

The Great Task: Life Review

The primary psychological work of later life is the "life review." It is a natural, often unconscious process of looking back over one's life, of sifting through memories, accomplishments, failures, joys, and sorrows. This is not simply reminiscing; it is an active process of meaning-making. The individual grapples with the life they have lived and seeks to find a sense of coherence and wholeness in it. As they confront their own mortality, they ask the ultimate question: *Was my life a meaningful one?*

The Path to Integrity

Successfully navigating the life review stage leads to a state of integrity. This is the acceptance of one's life as it was lived, without overwhelming regret. It is the feeling that one's existence had purpose and made a contribution, however small, to the larger fabric of life. A person who achieves integrity does not fear death, but sees it as the natural conclusion to a complete life.

This sense of integrity is often expressed through a focus on legacy, which might be a literal legacy of family and grandchildren, or might be found in mentoring younger generations, volunteering, or passing on hard-won wisdom. For others, it is the freedom to pursue passions they never had time for before—art, learning, travel. They have, as the poet Rudyard Kipling wrote, learned to "meet with Triumph and Disaster / And treat those two impostors just the same." Their accumulated life experience can give them a unique form of emotional resilience and a "live and let live" perspective.

The Risk of Despair

If, however, the life review leads to a deep sense of regret, missed opportunities, and unresolved conflicts, the individual may fall into a state of despair—the feeling that time is now too short to try another path to integrity. The older person may be overwhelmed by bitterness, contempt for others, and a profound fear of death. The losses that often accompany aging—the death of a spouse, siblings, and friends; the decline in physical health—can feel unbearable without a grounding sense of purpose.

Psychoanalytic work with the elderly often reveals that despair in this stage is linked to unresolved conflicts from earlier developmental stages. Techniques like life review therapy can be enormously helpful, allowing an individual to reframe past experiences and reshape their personal narrative into one that is more coherent and accepting. The goal is not to erase regret, but to integrate it into a larger story of a life that was, for all its imperfections, their own.

What Can Be Done?

Fostering a sense of integrity and purpose is the key to well-being in later life. This is an active process that can be supported by individuals, families, and communities.

- **Encourage Storytelling and Reminiscence.** The life review is a natural process that can be actively encouraged. Ask an older loved one to tell you stories from their past. Use old photo albums as prompts. Consider recording an oral history for the family. This validates their life experiences and reinforces their sense of identity and legacy.
- **Create Roles of Purpose.** Retirement can leave a void once filled by a career. It is crucial to find new sources of purpose. This could involve formal mentoring programs, volunteering for a cause the individual believes in, or taking on a specific role within the family, such as the designated "story reader" for grandchildren.
- **Facilitate Intergenerational Connections.** One of the most powerful antidotes to both isolation and despair is connection with younger generations. Regular interaction keeps older adults feeling valued, relevant, and connected to the future. This is a profound win-win, as the wisdom of the older generation is an invaluable resource for the young.
- **Reframe Aging as Growth.** Actively challenge the cultural narrative of aging as decline. Frame it instead as a period of potential growth, wisdom, and reinvention. Celebrate new hobbies, new learning, and new friendships. This shift in perspective can profoundly impact how an individual experiences their later years.

Key Neuroscience Concepts

- *Neuroplasticity in Later Life:* The hopeful neurological principle that the brain can continue to form new connections and learn throughout the entire lifespan. This provides the biological basis for continued personal growth, learning, and adaptation in old age.
- *The Neurology of Wisdom:* The idea that a lifetime of experience creates highly refined and efficient neural pathways for emotional regulation. This allows many older adults to approach challenges with a level of calm and perspective that is often difficult for the more volatile adolescent or young adult brain.

Key Psychoanalytic Concepts

- *Integrity vs. Despair (Erikson):* The final and culminating psychosocial crisis of life. It involves a "life review" during which an individual confronts the totality of their existence. A sense that one's life was meaningful and well-lived leads to a state of integrity, while a life viewed with significant regret leads to despair.
- *Generativity and Legacy:* A key component of achieving integrity in later life. It involves a shift in focus from personal ambition to contributing to the well-being of future generations through mentoring, storytelling, volunteering, or nurturing family.
- *Reminiscence as Therapeutic Work:* The understanding that the process of looking back, telling stories, and making sense of one's past is not idle nostalgia, but vital and active psychological work necessary to integrate one's identity and find peace.

Chapter 19 References

Erikson, E. H., & Erikson, J. M. (1998). *The life cycle completed (Extended version)*. W. W. Norton & Company.

Kipling, R. (1910). *If—*.

Butler, R. N. (1963). The life review: An interpretation of reminiscence in the aged. *Psychiatry, 26*(1), 65–76.

A Call To Action

This book has laid out the psychological and neurological stakes. We have seen how the digital world can undermine trust, empathy, and even the construction of the self. Yet we have also seen that the brain is plastic, and that change is possible. We are not powerless. By demanding systemic reform, strengthening our communities, and making conscious choices in our own lives, we can begin to loosen the grip of social media. We can reclaim our minds, our children's, and our aging parents', mending the fractures the machine has left between us. The time to act is now.

Part 1 Toolkit

Practical Strategies for Parents, Caregivers, and Professionals

(Infants and Young Children, 0–7 years)

This toolkit provides concrete, evidence-based strategies to protect and nurture the foundational development of infants and young children in a world saturated with screens. It includes guidance for parents, caregivers, and professionals who support families during these early years.

Early childhood is a period of explosive brain growth, shaped moment by moment through relationships. The neuroscience of synaptic pruning and myelination, paired with the psychoanalytic insights of Winnicott, Bowlby, and others, makes clear that presence and connection are the bedrock of healthy development. This toolkit translates those insights into everyday practices, giving parents, caregivers, and professionals practical ways to nurture resilience and reduce the intrusion of screens during these foundational years.

A Toolkit for Parents and Caregivers

Creating a Connected Environment

- **Declare Sacred Spaces.** Designate areas of your home as permanently screen-free. The two most important are the child's bedroom and the family dinner table. A bedroom should be a sanctuary for sleep and stories, not a media center.
- **Establish Tech-Free Times.** Create rhythms in your day during

which screens are absent. The first hour of the morning and the last hour before bed are especially important. Screen use before bed disrupts melatonin production and harms sleep quality. **Audit Your Push Notifications.** The constant pings from phones are designed to hijack attention. Go through your phone settings and turn off all nonessential notifications.

Prioritizing Presence

- **Master the "Serve and Return."** When your child "serves" (points, babbles, asks a question), return the serve with words, eye contact, and warmth. This back-and-forth is the foundation of all future learning.
- **Be a "Sportscaster."** Narrate your day, especially with preverbal infants ("I'm putting on your red socks now." "Do you hear that dog barking outside?"). This narration surrounds your child with rich language.
- **Schedule "Do Nothing" Time.** Resist the urge to fill every moment. Boredom is the incubator of creativity. Undirected time allows children to explore their thoughts and invent their own games.

Mindful Media Consumption

- **Delay, Delay, Delay.** For children under 2, the optimal amount of solo screen time is zero. The only exception is interactive video chatting with loved ones.
- **Co-View, Don't Just Co-Exist.** For preschoolers (ages 2 to 5), if you choose to introduce screen media, make it a shared activity. Watch with them, ask questions, and use the content as a springboard for conversation.
- **Choose Content Carefully.** Look for high-quality, slow-paced educational programming from trusted sources like PBS Kids. Avoid content with rapid scene changes or distracting visuals.

A Guide for Professionals

For Pediatricians and Family Doctors

- Make conversations about media use a routine part of well-child visits. Ask nonjudgmentally about screen-time habits.
- Prescribe playful real-world interactions as essential "medicine" for development.

For Therapists and Mental Health Clinicians

- Observe family interaction patterns for technoference.
- Help parents explore the unconscious reasons for device use.
- Explicitly teach relational repair: how to apologize after distraction and restore connection.

For Early Childhood Educators

- Create a screen-free haven in the classroom.
- Educate parents gently on the science behind your play-based approach.
- Partner with families around the shared goal of helping their child thrive.

The earliest years offer both the greatest vulnerability and the greatest opportunity. By protecting sacred spaces for connection and restoring the rhythms of play, language, and presence, caregivers and professionals can lay the groundwork for empathy, self-regulation, and trust that will sustain children across their lifespan.

Part 1 Toolkit References

American Academy of Pediatrics. (2016). *Media and Young Minds. Pediatrics, 138*(5), e20162591.

American Psychological Association. (2025, June 9). Screen time and emotional problems in kids: A vicious circle? [Press release]. https://www.apa.org/news/press/releases/2025/06/screen-time-problems-children

Center on the Developing Child at Harvard University. (n.d.). *Serve and return.* https://developingchild.harvard.edu/science/key-concepts/serve-and-return/

Christakis, D. A. (2014). The effects of fast-paced cartoons on children's executive function.

Pediatrics, 133(4), 861–866. https://doi.org/10.1542/peds.2013-3356

Dworak, M., Schierl, T., Bruns, T., & Strüder, H. K. (2007). Impact of a 2-hour-long laptop-use on the sleep behavior and sleep EEG of adolescents. *Journal of Adolescent Health, 41*(6), 610–615. https://doi.org/10.1016/j.jadohealth.2007.05.004

Radesky, J. S., & Christakis, D. A. (2016). Increased screen time: Implications for early childhood development and behavior. *Pediatric Clinics of North America, 63*(5), 827–839. https://doi.org/10.1016/j.pcl.2016.06.002

Radesky, J., & Mendelsohn, A. L. (2019). The relationship between technoference and child well-being: A systematic review. *Pediatric Clinics of North America, 66*(2), 333–345. https://doi.org/10.1016/j.pcl.2018.12.006

Zhou, S., Ding, W., Xiao, B., & Li, Y. (2024). Screen time and behavioural problems among preschool children: Unveiling the mediating effect of sleep quality. *Early Child Development and Care, 1*(1), 1–15. https://doi.org/10.1080/03004430.2024.2393413

American Academy of Pediatrics. (n.d.). *Family media plan.* HealthyChildren.org. https://www.healthychildren.org/English/media/Pages/default.aspx

Siegel, D. J., & Bryson, T. P. (2011). *The whole-brain child: 12 revolutionary strategies to nurture your child's developing mind.* Bantam Books. Common Sense Media. (n.d.). *Digital citizenship & education.* https://www.commonsensemedia.org/digital-citizenship

Turkle, S. (2015). *Reclaiming conversation: The power of talk in a digital age.* Penguin Books. Center on Media and Child Health. (n.d.). *Media and child health clinician toolkit.* http://cmch.tv/clinicians

American Psychological Association. (2017). *Multicultural guidelines: An ecological approach to context, identity, and intersectionality.* https://www.apa.org/about/policy/multicultural-guidelines.pdf

Fairplay for Kids. (n.d.). *For parents.* https://fairplayforkids.org/for-parents/

Part 2 Toolkit

Practical Strategies for Parents, Caregivers, and Professionals

(Tweens and Adolescents, 8–18 years)

This toolkit offers practical strategies for parents navigating the complex years of tween and adolescent development in the digital age. At this stage, the role of parents shifts from direct control to coaching and collaboration, helping teens build the internal skills needed to thrive both online and offline. Professionals working with youth also play a vital role in supporting families.

Adolescence is often called a second birth of the brain. The limbic system surges ahead while the prefrontal cortex lags behind, and Erikson's search for identity takes center stage.

Screens magnify both the promise and the peril of this developmental window, amplifying comparison, risk-taking, and anxiety while offering new avenues for connection. This toolkit provides strategies for parents and professionals to help teens harness their strengths, build resilience, and navigate crises with support and compassion.

Strategies for Supporting Healthy Brain Development

- **Build the Brakes.** Counteract the "gas pedal" of the adolescent limbic system by strengthening the "brakes" of the prefrontal cortex. Encourage activities that require long-term focus and delayed gratification such as learning a musical instrument, training for a sport, or practicing mindfulness.

- **Protect Sleep Ruthlessly.** The bedroom must be a screen-free sanctuary. Enforce a family-wide rule that all devices are charged overnight in a central location outside of bedrooms. This is often the hardest, but most important, rule to protect mental health and academic performance.
- **Explain Their Brain.** Talk to teens about the "gas pedal and brakes" model of their brain. Framing impulsivity and risk-taking as part of normal development empowers them to manage it rather than feeling defective.

Strategies for Fostering a Strong Identity

- **Encourage an "Identity Portfolio."** Self-worth is built from real-world competence, not online "likes." Support offline activities that develop resilience and identity such as part-time jobs, volunteer work, school clubs, or sports.
- **Become a Media Literacy Mentor.** Talk openly about social media. Ask questions that build critical thinking: "Why do you think people only post perfect photos?" "What is this app's business model?"
- **Champion Solitude.** Normalize time alone without devices. Encourage solitary hobbies such as reading, drawing, or journaling. Frame downtime as an opportunity for creativity, not boredom.

Strategies for Family Harmony

- **Create a Family Tech Plan, Together.** Collaboratively create rules around technology. Involving teens in the process increases buy-in and reduces conflict.

- **Practice Co-Regulation, Not Control.** Shift from commands to collaboration. Instead of yelling, "Get off that game!" give a warning and calmly remind them of the family plan. Work together on solutions.
- **Use Their World as a Bridge.** Show curiosity about their digital lives. Ask them to explain a TikTok trend or show you a favorite game. Sharing in their world strengthens trust and communication.

First Aid Toolkit for Teens in Crisis

Adolescents sometimes face serious challenges from their online lives, including anxiety, cruelty, exploitation, and even suicidal thoughts. These strategies offer immediate, practical responses for parents and caregivers.

First Aid for Anxiety and an Overwhelmed State

- **Validate, Then Investigate.** Always begin with validation: "That sounds stressful" or "I can see why that upset you." Once your teen feels heard, you can gently explore the facts.
- **Enforce a Digital Curfew.** The hour before bed is when the anxious brain is most vulnerable. Make a nonnegotiable rule: all screens away one hour before bedtime.
- **Introduce "Worry Time."** Schedule 15 minutes daily for your teen to write down or talk through their worries. This practice helps contain anxiety so it doesn't overwhelm the entire day.

First Aid for Empathy Deficits and Online Cruelty

- **Shift from "What" to "Who."** When discussing online drama, focus on the people involved ("How do you think he felt?"). This trains empathy.

- **Assign Empathy Homework.** Encourage one daily act of kindness, such as giving a compliment or checking in on a peer.
- **Practice "Curiosity First."** Coach your teen to replace accusatory messages ("Why are you ignoring me?") with curiosity ("Hey, is everything okay?"). This defuses many conflicts.

First Aid for Cyberbullying and Exploitation

- **Document, Block, Report.** Teach your teen to screenshot harassment, block bullies, and report them to platforms and schools.
- **No-Shame Safety Plan.** Tell your teen explicitly, "If you are ever threatened online, you will not be punished. My first priority is your safety." This amnesty increases the chance they'll come to you for help.

When to Seek Professional Help

Seek immediate help from a therapist, counselor, or pediatrician if you notice:

- Persistent changes in sleep, eating, or hygiene.
- Complete withdrawal from friends and activities.
- A sharp, sustained drop in academic performance.
- Intense mood swings or prolonged irritability and sadness.
- Any mention of self-harm or suicide. Treat every disclosure as serious and urgent.

If your child is in immediate danger, go to an emergency room or call a suicide prevention hotline.

A Guide for Professionals

For Pediatricians and Family Doctors

- Make screen time a "vital sign" at well-child visits. Ask about usage nonjudgmentally and provide guidance.
- Prescribe play as medicine for language delays or behavior issues. Example: Spend 15 minutes a day on the floor with your child, phones away. Let them lead the play.
- Provide simple resources, such as one-page handouts with AAP screen-time guidelines.

For Therapists and Mental Health Clinicians

- Observe parent-child patterns during sessions. If a parent constantly checks their phone, discuss it as a dynamic, not just a behavior.
- Explore the "why" behind parent device use, including anxiety, stress, or unresolved neglect.
- Teach relational repair. Role-play apologies and reconnection after moments of distraction.

For Educators

- Create screen-free classrooms that emphasize sensory learning, imaginative play, and peer interaction.
- Educate parents gently about why screen-free and play-based approaches support development.
- Partner with parents around the shared goal of helping children thrive, rather than criticizing their habits.

Though the digital world can intensify adolescent struggles, it also offers opportunities to teach empathy, self-regulation, and critical thinking. When parents, educators, and clinicians place the emphasis on connection rather than control, they create the secure base teens need in order to explore, experiment, and ultimately grow into adults capable of using technology consciously rather than being consumed by it.

Part 2 Toolkit References

American Psychological Association. (2025, June 9). Screen time and emotional problems in kids: A vicious circle? [Press release]. https://www.apa.org/news/press/releases/2025/06/screen-time-problems-children

Christakis, D. A., Zimmerman, F. J., DiGiuseppe, D. L., & McCarty, C. A. (2007). Early television exposure and subsequent attentional problems in children. *Pediatrics, 120*(5), 990–996. https://doi.org/10.1542/peds.2007-0683

Hinduja, S., & Patchin, J. W. (2020). *Cyberbullying identification, prevention, and response: A manual for school administrators, mental health professionals, and law enforcement.*

Cyberbullying Research Center.

Radesky, J. S., & Mendelsohn, A. L. (2019). The relationship between technoference and child well-being: A systematic review. *Pediatric Clinics of North America, 66*(2), 333–345. https://doi.org/10.1016/j.pcl.2018.12.006

Siegel, D. J. (2010). *The mindful brain: Reflection and attunement in the cultivation of well-being.* W. W. Norton & Company.

Siegel, D. J., & Bryson, T. P. (2014). *No-drama discipline: The whole-brain way to calm the chaos and nurture your child's developing mind.* Bantam Books.

Zhou, S., Ding, W., Xiao, B., & Li, Y. (2024). Screen time and behavioural problems among preschool children: Unveiling the mediating effect of sleep quality. *Early Child Development and Care, 1*(1), 1–15. https://doi.org/10.1080/03004430.2024.2393413

Part 3 Toolkit

Practical Strategies for Adults and the Elderly

(Midlife through Later Life)

This toolkit offers practical strategies tailored to the challenges of adulthood and aging in the digital era. It includes ways to balance work and personal life, nurture relationships, support older adults in using technology safely, and build psychological resilience against digital manipulation.

Adulthood and aging bring their own challenges in the digital era. For adults, screens threaten work-life balance, intimacy, and focus. For older adults, they can deepen isolation or become tools of empowerment, depending on how they are used. Across the lifespan, the plasticity of the brain and the resilience of the psyche remain powerful allies. This toolkit offers strategies for midlife balance, elder well-being, and cultivating psychological resilience against digital manipulation.

Strategies for Adults in Midlife

- **Create a "Digital Commute."** For those working from home, the absence of a commute can blur the boundary between work and personal life. Establish rituals that bookend the day, such as a 15-minute walk before starting and after finishing work. This signals to the brain that the workday is over.

- **Schedule "Analog" Time with Your Partner.** If screens are straining a relationship, set recurring tech-free rituals: a nightly walk, a weekly game night, or Sunday coffee together. Treat these moments as nonnegotiable, like any work meeting.
- **Use Dating Apps with Intention.** If dating online, set clear limits. Use apps for a set period (20–30 minutes), then log off. Prioritize moving promising conversations into the real world quickly to avoid endless superficial texting.
- **Reclaim Your Bedroom.** Keep the bedroom for sleep and intimacy only. Use a physical alarm clock and charge devices in another room. This single change can improve sleep quality and rekindle connection with a partner.

Strategies for the Elderly

- **Encourage Storytelling and Reminiscence.** Invite older adults to share their stories. Use photo albums as prompts. This validates their experiences and reinforces identity and legacy.
- **Promote Lifelong Learning.** The brain remains plastic into old age. Encourage new skills—learning a language, trying a class, or picking up a hobby. This builds cognitive reserve and combats decline.
- **Prioritize Safety with Digital Literacy.** Offer classes on online safety for seniors. Teach them to spot scams and phishing attempts. This builds confidence and reduces vulnerability.
- **Use Tech as a Bridge, Not a Destination.** Video calls and social media should serve as stepping stones to real-world contact, not replacements. Help older adults use screens to maintain relationships and schedule in-person visits.
- **Simplify and Secure Devices.** Configure devices with large fonts, simplified interfaces, and preprogrammed contacts. Add security features to reduce frustration and prevent exploitation.

Strategies for Resilience and Reclaiming Reality

The digital world does not only affect children. Adults, too, must actively resist the pull of misinformation, addictive algorithms, and fragmented attention. These strategies support psychological resilience and brain health.

Psychological Resilience

- **Practice Perspective-Taking.** Before reacting to a shocking post, pause and consider *What experiences might have led them to this belief?* This builds empathy and interrupts primitive defenses like splitting. Splitting is a defense mechanism where a person views people or situations in extremes—either all good or all bad.
- **Name That Defense.** When feeling reactive, identify the defense mechanism at play. Is it denial, projection, or acting out? Naming it brings unconscious processes into awareness.
- **Log Off to Process.** When emotionally triggered, step away from the screen. Walk, talk to someone, or take time to process feelings before responding.

Reclaiming Reality

- **Perform a Feed Audit.** Regularly check who and what you follow. Add credible journalists, scientists, and thinkers with diverse perspectives to inoculate yourself against echo chambers.
- **Verify Before You Amplify.** Make it a rule to never share or "like" information without verifying it through a credible primary source. Teach teens to do the same.
- **Prioritize In-Person Dialogue.** Talk about divisive topics face-to-face whenever possible. Nonverbal cues and shared humanity help correct distortions and projections.

Rewiring the Brain

- **Embrace Novelty.** Learning new skills or trying new experiences strengthens neural pathways. Even small shifts—taking a new route, cooking a new recipe—can stimulate the brain.
- **Prioritize Focused Attention.** Neuroplasticity requires focus. Whether learning an instrument or meditating, single-tasking drives change.
- **Get Moving and Get Sleep.** Exercise and rest are nonnegotiable. Physical activity boosts BDNF, supporting neuron growth, while sleep consolidates learning.

A Personal and Public Call to Action

- At the Societal Level: Advocate. Support tech regulation and organizations like the Center for Humane Technology.
- At the Community Level: Lead by Example. Promote media literacy in schools and model balanced tech habits at home.
- At the Individual Level: Be Mindful. Track your own habits, turn off unnecessary notifications, and use apps intentionally rather than reflexively.

Even in later life the brain retains its capacity to adapt and grow. By using technology with intention, reclaiming in-person connection, and strengthening habits of focus and empathy, adults and elders alike can resist the fragmenting pull of the digital world. The task is not simply survival in an age of screens, but the ongoing reclamation of presence, meaning, and authentic human connection.

Part 3 Toolkit References

An, B. (2022). The digital divide and social isolation among older adults. *Journal of Gerontology: Social Sciences, 77*(3), 450–462. https://doi.org/10.1093/geronb/gbab171 American Psychological Association. (2024, May 15). The effects of social media on adult romantic relationships. [Press release]. https://www.apa.org/news/press/releases/2024/05/social-media-romantic-relationships

Cacioppo, S., Cacioppo, J. T., & Boomsma, D. I. (2020). The role of social media in loneliness and social isolation: A systematic review. *Journal of the American Medical Association, 323*(20), 2056–2065. https://doi.org/10.1001/jama.2020.6698

Doidge, N. (2007). *The brain that changes itself: Stories of personal triumph from the frontiers of brain science.* Viking.

Ekman, P. (2003). *Emotions revealed: Recognizing faces and feelings to improve communication and emotional life.* Times Books.

Haidt, J. (2012). *The righteous mind: Why good people are divided by politics and religion.* Pantheon Books.

Kouider, S., & Dehaene, S. (2007). Levels of processing during sleep: Toward a theory of the sleeping brain. *Trends in Cognitive Sciences, 11*(11), 485–493.

National Council on Aging. (n.d.). *Internet safety tips for older adults.* Retrieved from https://www.ncoa.org/economic-security/money-management/online-safety/internet-safety-tips-f or-older-adults/

Neustadt, R. (2018). The psychology of fake news and misinformation. *Journal of Social Psychology, 158*(5), 585–597.

Radesky, J. S., & Mendelsohn, A. L. (2019). The relationship between technoference and child well-being: A systematic review. *Pediatric Clinics of North America, 66*(2), 333–345. https://doi.org/10.1016/j.pcl.2018.12.006

Siegel, D. J. (2010). *Mindsight: The new science of personal transformation.* Bantam Books.

Tversky, A., & Kahneman, D. (1974). Judgment under uncertainty: Heuristics and biases. *Science, 185*(4157), 1124–1131.

Wills, C. E., & D'Andrea, J. D. (2019). The digital commuter: Strategies for work-life integration in the mobile office. *Human Relations, 72*(8), 1324–1345. https://doi.org/10.1177/0018726718818818 Zhou, S., Ding, W., Xiao, B., & Li, Y. (2024). Screen time and behavioural problems among preschool children: Unveiling the mediating effect of sleep quality. *Early Child Development and Care, 1*(1), 1–15. https://doi.org/10.1080/03004430.2024.2393413

Conclusion

We began this book with a warning: that the ways our digital devices shape our lives can be a matter of life and death. We have journeyed through the full arc of human development, from the cradle to the grave, to illustrate how this is not hyperbole, but a profound and pervasive truth.

Through the dual lenses of psychoanalysis and neuroscience we have seen how the architecture of the modern digital world is often fundamentally at odds with the architecture of a healthy human mind.

We saw how the "present-but-absent" parent, distracted by a screen, can fail to provide the consistent, attuned care an infant needs to develop basic trust. We explored how the passive consumption of screens can hijack the essential work of childhood—play and language—and how the device can emerge as a "new third," a rival for parental love that can warp a child's internal model for relationships.

For the adolescent, we saw a "neurological mismatch"—a brain with a fully developed emotional engine and unreliable brakes—colliding with a digital environment engineered to exploit that very vulnerability. We saw how the search for identity can be distorted by the curated, false mirrors of social media and how the data void of online communication can become a breeding ground for projection, paranoia, and a tragic deficit of empathy.

In adulthood, we saw how these patterns can persist, fueling addictions, eroding intimacy, and creating a state of chronic distraction that inhibits focus and rest. And for the elderly, we saw how the screen presents a double-edged sword: a potential lifeline against the pain of isolation, but also a vector for scams, sedentary behavior, and anxiety.

The mechanisms of this damage are now clear. It is the hijacking of our dopamine-based reward systems, the starving of our mirror neuron system, the algorithmic promotion of our most primitive defense mechanisms, and the systematic fracturing of a shared, fact-based reality.

Yet this book is not intended as a prophecy of doom. It is a call to awareness and a testament to hope. The same principle of neuroplasticity that allows the brain to be shaped by distraction also ensures that it can be reshaped by intention. The human psyche, which can be wounded by ruptured connections, also possesses a profound capacity for relational repair. The ultimate lesson is not that technology is inherently evil, but that our humanity is profoundly precious—and requires protection.

The solution is not to smash our smartphones and retreat from the modern world. The solution is to reclaim our agency. It is the conscious choice to put the phone down when a child speaks to us. It is the courage to teach our teens to think critically about the information they consume. It is the wisdom to prioritize the messy, inconvenient, and deeply nourishing reality of embodied human connection over the frictionless ease of the digital feed. The challenges are immense, but our capacity for love, presence, and conscious choice is greater. The work of building a more humane technology and a more connected society begins now—in our homes, in our communities, and in the quiet, deliberate choices we make every single day.

Epilogue

As clinicians, we spend our days listening to stories. We listen to stories of pain and loss, hope and resilience, the quiet struggles and profound triumphs that make up a human life. We wrote this book because we had begun to hear the same story over and over again, from patients of all ages. It was a story of disconnection—from others, from the world, and most troublingly, from themselves. And at the center of that story, almost always, was a glowing screen.

We watched as the timeless challenges of human development were amplified and distorted by this new, pervasive force. The infant's need for an attuned gaze, the toddler's drive for mastery, the adolescent's search for identity, the adult's desire for intimacy, the elder's quest for integrity—all of these were being complicated in new and alarming ways. The principles of psychoanalysis gave us a language for understanding the psychological meaning of these disruptions, while the findings of neuroscience provided a stark picture of the effects on the brain itself.

The technological landscape will continue to change at a speed we can barely comprehend. The rise of artificial intelligence and immersive virtual worlds will present a new generation of challenges that we can only begin to imagine. But what will not change are the fundamental needs of the human heart.

No algorithm can replace a parent's hug. No virtual reality can substitute for the feeling of shared laughter with a dear friend. No amount of online followers can cure the ache of loneliness. The core message of Disconnected Together is not anti-technology but pro-human. It is a defense of presence, an argument for empathy, and a plea to remember what is most essential.

Our greatest hope is that this book serves as a map for families trying to navigate this new territory. We hope it empowers you to set boundaries, to have difficult conversations, and to carve out sacred, screen-free space for your connections to flourish. Because in the end, when we look back on our lives, we will not remember the clever tweet, the viral video, or the number of "likes" we received. We will remember the faces of those we loved, the moments of genuine presence we shared, and the feeling of being truly seen and understood. That is the only reality that has ever truly mattered.

About the Authors

Harry Gill, MD, PhD, is a physician, entrepreneur, and neuroscience PhD who has devoted his career to helping people, particularly teenagers, overcome mental health challenges.

In his over two decades of clinical practice, Dr. Gill has directly overseen the treatment for hundreds of patients whose psychiatric conditions range in severity from mild to life-threatening. In that time, he has seen how the constant barrage of digital information and imagery erodes genuine human connection and leads to feelings of isolation and despair. It's here, in the raw and often heartbreaking narratives of his patients, that Dr. Gill found the impetus for this book.

Today, Dr. Gill is a board-certified psychiatrist, an Assistant Clinical Professor at George Washington University, and the president of HGMD, LLC, a private clinical psychiatry practice in New York City. He also serves as the Medical Director for Embark Behavioral Health, a nationwide mental health network, in Cabin John, Maryland, New York City, and Atlanta, Georgia.

Dr. Gill's interactions with hundreds of young individuals grappling with the fallout of digital immersion have provided him with gut-wrenching insights into the destructive nature of uncurated screen time and social media. But he possesses the expertise, empathy, and entrepreneurial drive to do something more.

Disconnected Together: A Family's Guide to Reclaiming Connection in a Digital World is his attempt to reach a broader audience while making a lasting impact on those whose world is fragmented because of their inability to connect with other people.

Karyne Messina, EdD, is a psychologist, psychoanalyst, and author of eight books that use psychoanalytic concepts to explain real-world problems facing our society today. She is on the medical staff of Suburban Hospital, where she previously served as Director of Outpatient Mental Health, a Fellow of the American Board of Psychoanalysts, and a founding member of the American Psychoanalytic Association's Commission on Artificial Intelligence (CAI). She works with individuals and families across the lifespan.

Dr. Messina is a featured podcast host on the New Books Network (NBN), where she conducts in-depth interviews with authors of new books on psychology, mental illness, climate change, and more. She hosts two podcast series on the NBN and YouTube channels. One, titled "Psychoanalytic Perspectives on Racism in America," is sponsored by the American Psychoanalytic Association and features Dr. Felecia Powell-Williams as her co-host. The other, which she hosts with Dr. Gill, is called, "Brain Rot: What Our Screens Are Doing to Our Minds." Dr. Messina also writes a regular newsletter on Substack.

Dr. Messina is also writing a Routledge book series called "Psychoanalysis, Technology and the Future." She recently became a coeditor of *Psychoanalysis and Psychotherapy in China* with its founder, Dr. David Scharff. After a transitional year she will become the journal's full-time editor-in-chief.

Praise for *Disconnected Together*

This book offers a powerful and urgent message for our mental health in this digital age. With a brilliant synthesis of neuroscience and psychoanalysis, the authors provide a crucial map for understanding how our relationship with technology is reshaping our minds, our relationships, and our sense of self. They bravely confront the profound challenges of our screen-saturated world, from the erosion of family connection to the rise of mental health crises in youth.

From the moment we are born, our brains are wired for connection, shaped by the back-and-forth of human interaction. The authors masterfully illustrate how digital devices, with their endless feeds and instant gratification, can hijack this fundamental process, leading to a profound sense of disconnection. They take readers on a journey through the stages of human development, showing how screens can undermine a child's sense of trust, fragment an adolescent's identity, and create a state of chronic anxiety in adults.

Rooted in clinical experience and grounded in a rich understanding of human development, *Disconnected Together* is a call to reclaim what is most essential: our capacity for presence, empathy, and authentic connection. It is an indispensable guide for anyone who has ever felt overwhelmed by the digital world and a necessary blueprint for building a more connected future. The authors remind us that the human brain, with its remarkable plasticity, has the power to change, offering a message of hope that we can indeed rewire our minds and reclaim our lives from the machine.

—Robert M. Gordon, PhD, ABPP Diplomate in
Clinical Psychology and Psychoanalysis

A groundbreaking and brilliant literary work that takes the reader on a journey of the interconnectedness between psychoanalysis and neuroscience. It is a must-read for anyone who seeks to understand the impact of the digital age on brain health and human development. A round of applause for the writers for taking the important steps to educate and empower the public on how to take back time and own the value of relationships.

—Dr. Andre'a Watkins, MD/MPH, CEO and Owner, Culinary Psychiatrist FreedomMind Wellcare and Consulting LLC

In a world increasingly shaped by algorithms and artificial intelligence, this book is an essential and urgent antidote. It provides a clear and uncompromising examination of the psychological toll our screens have already taken, laying bare the human cost of a society that prioritizes digital engagement over genuine connection. The analysis of the erosion of empathy and the rise of digital paranoia shows that we are losing a vital part of our shared humanity. The authors' deep dive into how constant stimulation warps our minds and separates us from our authentic selves is a necessary and timely warning.

The book is informative, terrifying, and yet reassuring. Informative because it breaks down the phases of life, from infancy to senior, and how screen time negatively impacts them, using well-explained and relatable science and psychology. Terrifying in its use of real-world examples, such as when it explores a baby's difficulties with competing with a phone for a parent's critically important attention, or a teenager being encouraged to hurt themselves while scrolling, or a senior falling for an online scam. Reassuring as it provides advice, examples, and clear steps to break the destructive behavior at all ages.

It's an optimistic book as it explains that once a person clearly sees the problem, they can take action to reduce the harm. I appreciate that the book emphasizes the importance of individuals taking control of their time, energy, actions, and attention. It does provide suggestions for